Nelson's
Church Leader's Manual for Congregational Care

Kent Spann and David Wheeler,
General Editors

THOMAS NELSON
Since 1798

NASHVILLE   DALLAS   MEXICO CITY   RIO DE JANEIRO

Published in Nashville, Tennessee, by Thomas Nelson. Thomas Nelson is a trademark of Thomas Nelson, Inc.

Book design and composition by Upper Case Textual Services, Lawrence, Massachusetts.

Thomas Nelson, Inc., titles may be purchased in bulk for educational, business, fund-raising, or sales promotional use. For information, please e-mail SpecialMarkets@ThomasNelson.com.

Scripture quotations noted KJV are taken from the KING JAMES VERSION of the Bible.

Scripture quotations noted MSG are taken from *The Message* by Eugene H. Peterson. © 1993, 1994, 1995, 1996, 2000. Used by permission of NavPress Publishing Group. All rights reserved.

Unless otherwise noted, Scripture quotations are taken from the NEW KING JAMES VERSION. © 1982 by Thomas Nelson, Inc. Used by permission. All rights reserved.

Scripture quotations noted NIV are taken from the HOLY BIBLE: NEW INTERNATIONAL VERSION. © 1973, 1978, 1984 by International Bible Society. Used by permission of Zondervan Publishing House. All rights reserved.

Library of Congress Cataloging-in-Publication Data

978-1-4185-4357-0 Hardcover

Printed in the United States of America

1 2 3 4 5 6 RRD 13 12 11 10

Contents

Part Four: Implementation

Editor's Preface

When people say, "I'm not a pastor!" they usually mean that it is not their job, or they feel unqualified. Many of God's people in the pew feel inadequate or ill equipped to care for others, so they leave it to the "paid professionals." The result is the loss of a congregation of people God desires to use to touch others. Paid professionals did not care for the man lying on the road beaten and battered; it was a regular man (Luke 10:30–37). Paid professionals did not minister to others in the early church; it was the ordinary member of the congregation (Acts 2:42–47).

Thank you for picking up this book. You accept that God called every individual to care for others in the church and the community. You seek to better equip yourself to minister to others.

This book is not for the minister, although the minister can use and learn from it. There are many versions of minister's manuals on the market. This manual addresses the layperson. We provide resources for the person who works alongside the pastor to aid in the care of God's people. We write for the person thrust into the role of caring for people because of a tragedy or a crisis.

Part 1, "Caring God's Way," lays the spiritual foundation for a ministry of the laity in a congregation. Spiritual leadership is a key component for offering care even though the person may not have an "official" position of leadership.

Part 2, "Caring for God's People," looks at some of the general skills necessary for caring for those in need. Prayer is the linchpin in caring for people. Mentoring touches lives, while raising up future leaders and helpers. You will also learn how to witness. True healing cannot take place until there is spiritual healing. Finally, we provide some basic counseling skills. Not everyone is a professional counselor, but everyone counsels.

"Caring for Hurting People" looks at issues you may encounter when ministering to God's people. Basic tips for ministering to the person hurting follows a brief overview of each problem you may come across. At the end of most chapters is a list of Scriptures provided to help you minister to the hurting individual. The material provides you a beginning point.

The final part, "Developing a Ministry of Congregational Care," guides you in how to set up a congregational care ministry in your church. What pastor or staff member would not welcome a host of men and women who come alongside him or her to care for the many and varied needs of a modern-day congregation.

Thanks is not a big enough word to all the people who contributed to this resource book. They have shared from the wealth of their experience and knowledge. May God enlarge their ministries.

So without further ado, "let's minister."

Contributors

Mark Becton
Senior pastor of Grove Avenue Baptist Church in Richmond, VA.

>   Theology of Congregational Care
>   Spiritual Leadership

Steve Cahill
Ordained minister for twenty-seven years who served as a prison chaplain for twenty years.

>   Prison Ministry

Beth Chilcoat
Editor of her husband, David's, story of terminal illness titled *Nobody Tells a Dying Guy to Shut Up: An Account of God's Faithfulness*. She and David were married for thirty-seven years before his passing.

>   Terminal Illness

Richard Halcombe
Director of missions for Southern Baptist churches in central Ohio.

>   Developing a Ministry of Congregational Care

Scott Hawkins
Associate dean for the Division of Behavioral Sciences,

College of Arts and Sciences, Liberty University in Lynchburg, VA.

Counseling

Steve Hopkins
Leader of Bible teaching and leadership for the State Convention of Baptists in Ohio. He pastored for twenty-two years.

Investing for Impact

Mark R. Laaser
President of Faithful and True Ministries in Eden Prairie, MN.

Sexual Addiction

Fred Milacci
Dean of Academic Administration for the graduate school at Liberty University in Lynchburg, VA.

Ministering to Your Minister
Suffering

Elton L. Moose
Professional counselor and pastor in Springfield and Dublin, OH, who specializes in helping those with gender identity issues.

Same-Sex Attraction
Sexual Violence

James L. Smith
Professor of substance abuse counseling at Ohio Christian University in Circleville, OH, where he teaches graduate courses and workshops in pastoral care and counseling.

Mental Disorders
Substance Abuse

Cindy Spann
A registered nurse, a pastor's wife for twenty-six years, and a proud mother of three sons.

Eating Disorders

Kent Spann
Pastor of the Highland Baptist Church in Grove City, OH, and coeditor of *Nelson's Church Leader's Manual for Congregational Care*.

Conflict
Divorce
Grief
Hospital Ministry
Suicide

Kip Wahlquist
Founder of the nonprofit Christian counseling and consulting ministry Transforming Resources in Bloomington, MN.

Prayer Care

David Wheeler
Associate professor of evangelism, Liberty University and Liberty Baptist Theological Seminary in Lynchburg, VA, and coeditor of *Nelson's Church Leader's Manual for Congregational Care.*

> Becoming the Lay Minister God Wants You to Be
> God's Will
> Special Needs

Part One
Caring God's Way

Theology of Congregational Care

Mark Becton

At many church conventions or conferences, you are likely to find pastors huddled in a hallway wheezing with laughter. Most of the time, it is because they are telling stories on themselves. I was in one of those huddles when a pastor told this story.

He was in his early twenties, and was proud to be pastor of his first full-time church. The church was close enough for him to commute to seminary, which meant whatever he learned in class that week, his church learned too.

One semester he picked up a workbook on hospital visitation and thought it would be good to train his deacons. They met Thursday nights for the next eight weeks. But after the sessions were through, the pastor had learned more than he taught.

Midway through the training the brother of one of the deacons was in a serious farming accident and was flown to the hospital. One of the oldest deacons called the young pastor and said, "Preacher, he's at a hospital you've never been to, so I'll pick you up in my truck and we can go together."

The injured man's room was packed with nine or ten family members. Not long after introductions, the doctor stepped in to examine the wound. The man had been drilling a hole for a fence post, and his leg had been caught in an auger. His injury was hidden beneath a sheet. But when the doctor lifted the sheet to look at his leg, the young pastor decided to look as well.

Seeing the wound had a strange effect on the pastor. Immediately the room became small and very warm. Swaying like a strand of wheat in the wind, he knew if he didn't step out soon someone would have to carry him out. Leaning toward the older deacon who brought him, he whispered, "I need to step outside." Soon the older man followed and found his pastor leaning against the wall. He asked, "Are you all right, Preacher?" Trying to sound strong, he answered, "Sure. I'm fine." But then he began to slowly slide down the wall.

Thankfully, he saw a bay window not far away. The ledge of the bay window was actually an air-conditioning vent. Slowly walking to the vent, he sat on it so the cool air could bring color to his face. After a few minutes on the vent, the deacon walked over to his pastor and gently said, "Preacher, if you don't mind, I need to go home." That was his gracious way of saying, "Preacher, you look worse than the man we came to see."

The next time the pastor met with his deacons to train them in making hospital visits, he kept one eye on his notes and the other on the deacon who watched him nearly faint. Yet not once during the session did the deacon bring it up. However, when the pastor closed in prayer and the men started to file out, the old man spread an ornery smile and said, "Fellahs, let me suggest something. If you plan to make a hospital visit with our 'little' preacher, you might want to take this with you."

Out from his pocket he pulled a small bottle of smelling salts.

That story came to mind when I was asked to write a theology of congregational care. Writing a theology of congregational care means the information shared in this chapter comes straight from Scripture. Yet looking back over the years, I have been the pastor of many deacons and others like the old man in the truck. Though they may not have known where to find the chapter and verse in the Bible, they lived those truths and principles beautifully. They cared for so many without even knowing there was such a thing as a theology of congregational care.

Because you are holding this book, your heart for your pastor and God's people is probably like the man with the truck who had to help his pastor make a hospital visit. So on behalf of all the pastors you have helped and the people you have cared for, thank you.

Displaying God's Nature

Providing congregational care is more natural than most realize. When you care for others, you are displaying the nature of God within you. God reminds you of this each time you read Genesis 1:26–27.

> ²⁶ Then God said, "Let Us make man in Our image, according to Our likeness; let them have dominion over the fish of the sea, over the birds of the air, and over the cattle, over all

the earth and over every creeping thing that creeps on the earth." [27] So God created man in His own image; in the image of God He created him; male and female He created them.

Every builder, artist, sculptor, and song writer begins their creative work with a vision. Verse 26 uses two words to describe God's vision when He created you. He wanted to create you in His image and likeness.

God's Image and Likeness

The Hebrew word for *image* (tselem) refers to something cut. Like pagan religions cutting the image of their false gods into wood or stone, Almighty God cut his image into you. You are to be a living, breathing image of God. The Hebrew word for *likeness* (demut) comes from a root word meaning to resemble (damah).[1] Looking at how God uses these two words in verse 26, you learn something important. Though God cut you to be a walking and breathing image of him, you are not God. You are a resemblance of him. That resemblance is seen in your care for others.

You need to also remember that in Genesis 3, Adam and Eve sinned against God. Their sin marred God's image in them and in you and me. However, 2 Corinthians 3:17–18 explains how God is trying to transform you as a believer so that others can see in you what he originally intended. He wants to see, and wants others to see, His image in you. That transforming process involves cutting away the sin from you so others can see God's image. God's image in you can be seen clearly when you care for others.

God's Nature in His Instructions, the Psalms, and His Names

Again, caring for others should come naturally for the believer. It is a part of God's nature, and God's desire is for His nature to be seen in you.

One of the ways you see the caring quality of God is by reading the many biblical passages where He tells us to help those in need. You have read them many times, but did you realize that there are approximately forty references in Scripture where God charges his people to care for the orphans and fatherless. There are also roughly eighty references regarding the care for widows, and more than two hundred passages that call for meeting the needs of the poor. You even find verses that speak to helping the stranger and alien in your midst (Lev. 19:33–34; 24:17–22).

Yet the best place to capture God's caring nature is in the Psalms. Many are familiar with Psalm 23, but take a moment to read Psalm 146.

> [1] Praise the LORD!
>> Praise the LORD, O my soul!
> [2] While I live I will praise the LORD;
>> I will sing praises to my God while I have my being.
> [3] Do not put your trust in princes,

Nor in a son of man, in whom there is no
help.
4 His spirit departs, he returns to his earth;
In that very day his plans perish.
5 Happy is he who has the God of Jacob for his
help,
Whose hope is in the LORD his God,
6 Who made heaven and earth,
The sea, and all that is in them;
Who keeps truth forever,
7 Who executes justice for the oppressed,
Who gives food to the hungry.
The LORD gives freedom to the prisoners.
8 The LORD opens the eyes of the blind;
The LORD raises those who are bowed
down;
The LORD loves the righteous.
9 The LORD watches over the strangers;
He relieves the fatherless and widow;
But the way of the wicked He turns upside
down.
10 The LORD shall reign forever—
Your God, O Zion, to all generations.
Praise the LORD!

Old Testament scholar John Phillips calls the last five
psalms "Hallelujah Psalms." They resemble five doxolo-
gies at the end of the book of Psalms. It is believed that
Psalms 146–150 were written as praise pieces after the
completion of the second temple in 518 BC. Knowing

that our God is the God of extreme details, Phillips adds that it appears that these five psalms parallel the first five books of the Bible. That means Psalm 146 is the praise piece that reflects what is recorded in the book of Genesis.[2]

Though the psalm could have praised God for His faithfulness to Abraham, Isaac, Jacob, and Joseph, it focused its praise on God's nature. Not only is God praised for creating life (vv. 5–6), He is also praised for the way He cares for the lives He creates (vv. 7–9). There, you read that it is God's nature to provide justice for the poor, food to the hungry, freedom to the prisoners, sight to the blind, strength for the weak (raises those bowed down), love for the righteous, care to those who are alone (watches over the strangers), and relief to the fatherless and widows.

If you live your life consistently, in time you will be labeled for the life you live. That is true of God as well. Eleven times in Psalm 146 God is called "the LORD." It is the most reverent expression attributed to him in Scripture. In the Hebrew, it is the word *Jehovah* (*yhwh*). It means "I AM."

Yet throughout the Old Testament, God's caring nature caused other labels to be added. When speaking of God, God is called Jehovah Jireh (The Lord will provide, Gen. 22:14), Jehovah Rapha (The Lord that heals, Ex. 15:26), Jehovah Nissi (The Lord is my Banner/Refuge, Ex. 17:15), Jehovah Shalom (The Lord is peace, Judg. 6:24), and Jehovah Raah (The Lord is my Shepherd, Ps. 23). You cannot escape the cascading evidence of the caring nature of God, nor can you avoid the truth that since God created you in His image it is God's intent for His caring nature to be seen in you. However, some will avoid the opportunities to let God's nature be seen by claiming that such care is not their spiritual gift.

Nature Versus Giftedness

The argument of nature versus giftedness also surfaces in discussions about evangelism. Because Ephesians 4:11 states that God "gave some to be apostles, some prophets, some evangelists, and some pastors and teachers" many believers think they are to give the responsibility of sharing Jesus to the ones gifted at it—the evangelists. Therefore, it is also likely that some believers think that the responsibility of congregational care should be given to those gifted by God to do it.

Romans 12 and 1 Corinthians 12 list the spiritual gifts that God gives believers. You witnessed all these gifts in the person of Jesus. After Jesus' ascension to heaven, He gave those same gifts to His followers by placing his Spirit within them. Wisely though, Jesus divided His gifts among His followers so that we would have to work together and depend on Him to continue his ministry.

Among the spiritual gifts are the gifts of service, encouragement, and mercy. Sadly, there is the tendency to let those who have these gifts give all the congregational care. Like giving all the evangelism to the evangelists, not only does this distort God's plan, it also does not allow the passion and nature of God to come through you. By sharing your faith and by extending God's care you fulfill

God's desire for your life. You display his image and likeness. And when you fulfill God's desire for your life, you experience real fulfillment in life.

Thus the responsibility of congregational care, like evangelism, is not just for those who are gifted at it. It is for all who have surrendered their lives to Christ. As a follower of Jesus, you will find His Spirit prompting you to let the nature of God come through you in every opportunity you have to care for others.

Congregational care is not just for those with certain spiritual gifts. It is for every believer, for every believer has been created in the image of a caring God.

Sharing God's Care

There are times when the needs are more than one believer can meet. After my twenty-ninth birthday, I became the pastor of a church that was dear to me. My dad became pastor of this same church when I was three weeks old. Though we moved away when I was five, I still had fond memories of a wonderful childhood there.

Twenty-five years earlier, the church was a vibrant fellowship in a thriving suburb. The pictorial directory captured the faces of middle-aged, middle-income families, all excited about the future. Many of the members when Dad was pastor were still members when I became pastor. In fact, one older woman took me by the hand on my first Sunday and said, "Oh, I can't believe I changed the diaper of my pastor." A little embarrassed, I asked her to let that be our secret.

Twenty-five years later a lot had changed. The predominantly white, middle-class community was now becoming a patchwork of multicultural, lower-income families. In some ways the church had changed as well. It aged. The facilities were older as was the median age of the congregation. I soon learned that serving an older membership church in a changing community meant everyone had a need. And as their pastor, everyone expected me to meet his or her need. It was the first time I experienced the drain that comes when the care for a congregation and community is not shared.

The drain of caring for others can be hard to describe. The best description I found came from an older pastor who told me, "I feel like the lone milk cow in the pasture. I've got four teats and three of them are dry. I've got a line of calves all waiting their turn, and the calf that's on me now is punching me for more."

Basically, the pastor stated what many say when a congregation does not share in the care of one another. The common cry is "I have nothing left to give."

When you look at examples in the Old and New Testaments, you see God underscoring the importance of sharing the care of a congregation. It cannot be done by one individual, or even a few. It has to be the responsibility of all.

An Old Testament Example

The first example of the need for sharing congregational care appears in Exodus 18. Moses led the exodus from Egypt. With staff in hand, he marched out with two to three million of God's people following him. Though the initial exodus was wonderful, reality soon surfaced.

Consider what would be involved in relocating an entire metropolitan area. You are responsible for their basic needs of food and shelter as well as keeping the peace. It can be overwhelming, and it was for Moses. That is why, for Moses, there was no place like home. He led all two to three million Israelites to the wilderness near the home of his father-in-law, Jethro.

For several nights, Jethro watched Moses meet the needs of everyone. In Exodus 18:17–23, he told Moses what he saw and then made a recommendation to Moses.

> [17] So Moses' father-in-law said to him, "The thing that you do is not good. [18] Both you and these people who are with you will surely wear yourselves out. For this thing is too much for you; you are not able to perform it by yourself. [19] Listen now to my voice; I will give you counsel, and God will be with you: Stand before God for the people, so that you may bring the difficulties to God. [20] And you shall teach them the statutes and the laws, and show them the way in which they must walk and the work they must do. [21] Moreover you shall select from all the people able men, such as fear God, men of truth, hating covetousness; and place such over them to be rulers of thousands, rulers of hundreds, rulers of fifties, and rulers of tens. [22] And let them judge

the people at all times. Then it will be that every great matter they shall bring to you, but every small matter they themselves shall judge. So it will be easier for you, for they will bear the burden with you. [23] If you do this thing, and God so commands you, then you will be able to endure, and all this people will also go to their place in peace."

Jethro's assessment of Moses could be his assessment of many trying to care for others. If you keep doing it alone, you will wear yourself out. Furthermore, those you are trying to care for alone will grow tired of you for two reasons. Either you will not be able to get to their need in time, or even if you do get to them in time, you will not have anything left to give your best to their need.

Therefore, Jethro recommended that Moses train the people in God's ways (v. 20). God's people living God's ways will resolve most needs before they surface. Jethro also recommended that Moses select men of character who had the capability to meet most of the needs for Moses (v. 21). They brought the needs too great for them to handle to Moses (v. 22).

This was a wonderful solution for everyone. These men of character met needs more quickly and with greater care because no one person had to do it all. And as for those who provided the care, I am sure they were more fulfilled by the effort. They could give from the caring nature of God that was within them without the fear of having nothing left to give.

A New Testament Example

One of the wonderful attributes of God's Word is its detailed consistency. Lessons in the Old Testament often repeat in the New Testament. That is true of Acts 6. In some ways when you read Acts 6, it sounds as though you are reading Exodus 18. To appreciate what happened in Acts 6, you need to remember what transpired in Acts 1–5.

Much happened in the six months covered in Acts 1–6. It began with 120 of Jesus' confused and frightened followers huddled in an upper room in Acts 1. Obediently, they prayed for ten days. Then in Acts 2, the Holy Spirit used them in a dramatic way. Racing from their hiding place, they penetrated the tightly packed streets of Jerusalem and told all there about Jesus. On that day, 3,000 believed and were baptized. For the next six months the 3,000 continued talking about Jesus and more believed.

In Acts 6, as it was in Exodus 18, there were more needs than there were people to provide care. Thus, a tension rose within the church because there were too few members to meet all the widows' needs. The frustration over this threatened God's work. However, the apostles offered a remedy (in Acts 6:1–4 NIV). The remedy sounded similar to the one posed by Jethro in Exodus 18. This time, the solution came from the apostles.

6 ¹ In those days when the number of disciples was increasing, the Grecian Jews among them complained against the Hebraic Jews because their widows were being overlooked

in the daily distribution of food. ²So the Twelve gathered all the disciples together and said, "It would not be right for us to neglect the ministry of the word of God in order to wait on tables. ³Brothers, choose seven men from among you who are known to be full of the Spirit and wisdom. We will turn this responsibility over to them ⁴and will give our attention to prayer and the ministry of the word."

In case you missed them, let me point out the similarities between Acts 6 and Exodus 18. In both chapters a growing tension affected the leaders and the people. This tension threatened to stop God's work. Sounding like Jethro, the apostles stressed the importance of teaching God's people God's ways (Acts 6:2) because the apostles knew that understanding God's ways will address many needs before they surface. Also like Jethro, the apostles recommended that men with godly character and capabilities help meet the needs (Acts 6:3). Finally, with others focusing on the needs, the apostles could pray and give attention to weightier matters (Acts 6:4). That was what Jethro thought, when he made his suggestions to Moses in Exodus 18.

Do you remember the old pastor talking about being the lone milk cow in the pasture? With God's plan now explained by Jethro and the apostles, he would not have to worry about having nothing left to give, while others still waited for him to give more. He would no longer be the only milk cow in the pasture. And because others were having their needs met, he would actually enjoy, not dread, hearing someone say, "Pastor, could you help me with something?"

Leading Congregational Care

There is one more similarity shared between Acts 6 and Exodus 18. Both accounts emphasize that the leading helpers need to be men of character and capability. Jethro instructed Moses to look for men of truth who feared God and hated covetousness (Ex. 18:21). The apostles told the people to look for men full of the Holy Spirit and wisdom (Acts 6:3). There is an important principle to remember. Though every believer is to share the responsibilities in caring for others, those with additional responsibilities must bring more to the table.

You may remember that Jethro told Moses to give individuals responsibilities according to their abilities to fulfill them. This is why Moses charged some to care for only ten or more, while others could care for hundreds or even thousands (Ex. 18:21). This is likely the principle the apostles applied when they asked the people to select deacons to care for the needs of the widows. Can you imagine how many widows there would be in a church with 10,000 active members? Yet the apostles selected only seven men to meet this need. The apostles possibly thought seven would be enough if those seven enlisted and equipped others to help. That is why the apostles needed to be sure that the original seven were men of great character and capabilities. They would set the tone for the type of care given under their leadership.

By Acts 8, the church began to spread and multiply. God would use the apostle Paul to plant many new churches throughout the civilized world. Thus the idea used in Acts 6 became a more permanent part of church life. Deacons, or better translated with the word *servants*, became a God-ordained necessity for providing congregational care. In his letter to Timothy, Paul expanded on what Jethro told Moses and what the apostles first told the church. Paul described the qualities God requires of those who give leadership to congregational care. They are recorded in 1 Timothy 3:8–15.

God gives you a guide in performing character references for a job that is dear to Him when you read 1 Timothy 3:8–15. It is God's guide to discovering those who will give leadership to the care that is given to His church. According to God's guide, the individual needs to pass three character references.

Personal Character

When looking for someone to give leadership to congregational care, you first need to check the individual's personal character. Verse 8 explained, "Likewise deacons must be reverent, not double-tongued, not given to much wine, not greedy for money." Here, Paul identified specific qualities to look for when examining the personal character of a prospective deacon. Remarkably, each checkpoint began with the words "must not."

It has been said that character is not seen only in what a person is willing to do, but sometimes you see it best in what he or she is not willing to do. That may be why Paul initiated his character references by identifying what a caring leader "must not" do.

Paul wrote they "must not" be double-tongued. That means saying something one place and something different somewhere else. They were to be sincere men of their word. Second, Paul said they "must not" be addicted to wine. Because of the ongoing argument over drinking versus being drunk, or the debate whether or not the wine Jesus drank was fermented, remember what Paul wrote in Romans 14:21: "It is good neither to eat meat nor drink wine nor do anything by which your brother stumbles or is offended or is made weak." If it caused another to stumble, Paul charged, "Don't do it."

The final "must not" from Paul comes with the emphasis that deacons "must not" be greedy. This deals with ungodly pursuits, practices, and profits in business. Therefore, a deacon must not be involved in any of these activities.

Though the personal character references sound strict, many in the church will pass. It is important to remember that just because someone is respected in the community and in business may not mean that person will pass all of God's reference checks.

Theological and Spiritual Character

The second reference check involves examining the individual's spiritual and theological character. Paul explained in 1 Timothy 3:9 that the candidate needed to be seen "holding the mystery of the faith with a pure conscience." The word *holding* literally means "to keep tightening your grip." A deacon should always be tightening his grip on the "deep truths" (1 Tim. 3:9 NIV) of God. Like Moses learned from Jethro, and the first church learned from the apostles, many issues can be resolved by knowing and living by God's instructions. Therefore, it is crucial that deacons continue tightening their grip on the deep truths of God and living those truths with a pure conscience.

Proven Character

Tragically, there are those who can walk you through the Bible, yet they do not walk with the author. There are men who may know the rules of God but do not have a relationship with Him. People can be theologically straight but spiritually empty. That is why God looks for men to serve as deacons whose personal character is respectable, and whose theological and spiritual character is growing and commendable. The best way to be sure they have these traits is to make one last reference check. You need to look at their proven character.

Few areas will prove a man's character more than the way he loves and leads his family. Regarding this matter, Paul wrote in verses 10–13:

> [10] But let these also first be tested; then let them serve as deacons, being found blameless.
> [11] Likewise, their wives must be reverent, not

slanderers, temperate, faithful in all things.
[12] Let deacons be the husbands of one wife,
ruling their children and their own houses
well. [13] For those who have served well as deacons obtain for themselves a good standing
and great boldness in the faith which is in
Christ Jesus.

In verse 15, Paul described the church as God's
household—his family. Thus, before setting apart a deacon to care for God's family, Paul charged Timothy to
be sure the prospective deacon provided godly love and
care to his family.

Why Are the Requirements So Tough?

Though these seem like strict requirements for serving as a deacon, I believe God made them strict for the
following reasons. First, God did not want the church to
select deacons simply because they had a good business
sense. Deacons are not a board of directors who make
decisions for a business. In God's plan, deacons are a
group of servants who care for the needs of the body of
Christ.

Second, God wants deacons set apart on their own
merits. I have heard of churches saying, "Well, his father
and grandfather were deacons. It's only right that he
become a deacon." Though his dad and granddad may
have had the character to be deacons, it does not mean
the grandson does. A person's own character is the sole
basis for being considered a servant.

Third, God wants deacons who will serve, not sit. God wants proven servants who will keep doing what they have been doing because God and his people want to keep getting what they have been getting: true servants. When God's people receive godly care from servants with high character and capabilities, the benefits are astounding.

Reaping the Benefits of Congregational Care

Taking the initiative to meet the needs of your congregation is an extreme experience: extremely stressful and extremely rewarding. Several years ago, the National Institute of Occupational Safety and Health listed the thirty most stressful jobs. Second only to health technician was the job of waiter or waitress.[3] I have never held that job, but I can appreciate the stress of trying to meet three needs: the needs of the cook, the customer, and the owner or manager. According to Acts 6, providing congregational care means trying to meet three needs: the needs of the members, and by extension the ministers, and the kingdom.

Meeting the Needs of the Members

In Acts 1–5, the church exploded (see especially Acts 1:15; 2:41; 4:4). The members focused on making Jesus a part of their daily conversations. As a result, they added new believers each day. However, in Acts 6 the conversations changed. Instead of talking about Jesus outside the church, they talked to one another about a problem in the church. The church was not caring for Greek widows as well as the Jewish widows. As a result, the overall work of the church came to a stop until the need was met.

If given a choice whether they felt more fulfilled talking to others about Jesus or talking to one another about a problem, they would have chosen the former. That is why meeting the needs of church members can be so rewarding. Not only does helping someone with a problem fulfill you, but you and the fellow believer you helped are now excited to focus again on what fulfills you most: talking to others about Jesus.

Meeting the Needs of the Ministers

Congregational care also meets the needs of the ministers. In Acts 6, Peter told the church that if he and the other apostles met this need, they would neglect the greater need of prayer and the ministry of the Word. When the seven were chosen to help the widows, they also helped Peter.

Nothing has changed in God's plan since Acts 6. When believers do what they can do to meet the needs of their fellow followers, it enables the ministers to do what only they can do to meet needs as well: teach God's Word. And when ministers teach God's Word and the church obeys, there should be fewer needs to meet.

Meeting the Needs of the Kingdom

Helpers meeting the needs of the members and ministers addresses what is needed to continue spreading

God's kingdom. All because of a need in the church, the members stopped talking to others outside the church. Peter and the other apostles would have stopped ministering the Word to meet this need if others in the church did not resolve it. When the apostles selected the seven to meet the need, the believers returned to sharing Jesus and Peter returned to ministering the Word. As a result the kingdom of God began to spread again. This time, Acts 6:7 recorded that it spread even faster than before— all because everyone was doing their part to provide congregational care.

Opening the Eyes of the Lost

Another unforeseen benefit of congregational care is what it does to those watching from the outside. Jesus said in John 13:35, "By this all will know that you are My disciples, if you have love for one another." When a congregation sincerely cares for one another and meets one another's needs, it will catch the attention of an unbelieving world—especially when that same care is given to those in need outside the church.

The initial reaction after the birth of the church was awe. Acts 2:43 (NIV) recorded that "everyone was filled with awe." And why should they not be awed? Verses 44 and 45 explained how they took care of one another. Then verse 47 added something unusual. It stated that the church was enjoying "favor with all the people." When was the last time you heard people outside the church speaking favorably about the work of the church? They did in Acts 2 because the care that was given to those in the church was given to others outside the church as well.

In his article in *Christian History and Biography*, Princeton University sociologist Rodney Stark cites records indicating that in the years AD 165 and AD 251 two great plagues swept the Roman Empire. Each plague killed one-third of the empire's population, and with each plague, the believers impressed their community with their willingness to serve. Stark writes:

> The willingness of Christians to care for others was put on dramatic public display when two plagues swept the empire, one beginning in 165 and the second in 251. Mortality rates climbed higher than 30 percent. Pagans tried to avoid all contact with the afflicted, often casting the still-living into the gutters. Christians, on the other hand, nursed the sick, even though some believers died doing so.[4]

With believers so active in meeting the needs of nonbelievers, no wonder verse 47 ends with the affirming statement, "And the Lord added to the church daily those who were being saved."

Being Handy to God

Pastor, missionary, and author Tom Elliff often tells of his experience with his grandfather and the sobering lesson he learned about being handy to God.

While working with a piece of wood Tom's grandfather asked him to grab a certain tool off the wall. Unfamiliar with the tool, Tom hesitated until his grandfather said, "Tom, it's on the left." Moving to the left, but still uncertain, Tom's grandfather told him, "Tom, it's toward the top." Trying to decide which tool to grab, Tom heard his grandfather sigh, "That's okay, Tom. I've fixed it with this screwdriver." With the screwdriver still in his hand, Tom's grandfather shared the following lesson:

> Tom, there were other tools I could have used that were far better suited for the job. Do you want to know why I used this screwdriver? I used it because it was handy. Tom, there may be other, better individuals better suited for a particular job, but the one God will use is the one that is handy. Keep yourself handy to God.[5]

You and I will always think others are better suited for opportunities at the church or to meet a need in the community. God is not asking how well suited you are. He only wants to know if you will be handy. Those who are handy to God get to experience the fulfillment and joy of being used by God. Furthermore, you get to experience all the benefits that come with providing congregational care.

Spiritual Leadership
Mark Becton

I was nineteen years old and serving as a part-time youth pastor when a pastor very close to me gave me *Leadership Profiles from Bible Personalities*. Opening the glossy-covered book and fanning through the pages, I admit I was somewhat intrigued. I did not know books on leadership existed, much less leadership from a biblical perspective. Before I could ask why my mentor gave me the book, he told me and added a charge:

> I've been a pastor now for thirty years. One of the surprising things about leading people is that it's harder than you think. Oh, don't get me wrong; there are some fulfilling experiences when leading people. But it seems people are looking more and more for godly leaders these days. And it's not only harder to find one; it's harder to be one. Therefore, I'm giving you your first book on leadership and telling you that you need to pick up as many books on leadership as you can.

I took this valuable advice and began purchasing more books on leadership. I even graduated college with a minor in general business. But somewhere along the way the lines separating business leadership and spiritual leadership began to blur. Four years later, while serving as a pastor, I found myself sitting in committee meetings across from some seasoned business leaders. I am sure my eyes glossed over as I listened to them make decisions with such confidence. The voice of one particular man still echoes in my head. Encouraging the committee to make a hard decision, he said in an assuring tone, "I know it's a hard decision to make, but business is business." And the committee followed his lead.

Even at age twenty-three, the statement "business is business" did not sound right, especially when tied to making decisions at church. Thus for the next several years I was conflicted. I continued purchasing books on leadership. You know you can find one almost everywhere—in bookstores, airports, on the Internet. I even found one for sale at a carwash. Today with all the books, seminars, and corporate programs provided, leadership training has become a multibillion-dollar industry. Everyone is looking for leadership principles to help them at work. But how do those principles carry over with the most important work of all—God's work?

I carried this conflict within for nearly twenty years until I attended another leadership training conference for pastors. Fifty of us met for two or three days. During one of the sessions, one of the leaders told us that there may be successful business leaders and politicians in your church but that those folks were not called by God to be the pastor. And that did it. That statement took me back to the day I received *Leadership Profiles from Bible Personalities*. The challenge was not for me to read all the books on leadership to instill good business practices at church. All effective leadership principles are actually biblical principles. You can find them illustrated beautifully in the lives of many preserved in Scripture. I had gotten off track looking for leadership principles of business to apply at church. All the while God had preserved spiritual leadership principles in the Bible that not only help at church but also will influence your leadership at work and in life.

As you continue reading I hope that you will come to the same aha moment I did. I hope you will see that spiritual leadership is far different from any other form of leadership. You will also see that you can apply the principles of spiritual leadership to every facet of your life. However, when you do, you will realize something else as well. You will experience spiritual attacks that you never faced before, all because you are striving to be a spiritual leader.

Spiritual Leadership ... Is Different

You may be a natural leader. Your vision for what is needed, your drive to fulfill the vision, and your ability to inspire others to join the effort may energize you and even be easy for you. Yet because of your natural ability as a leader, you may quickly confuse natural leadership with spiritual leadership.

You may not be a natural leader. However, life has a way of putting you in places where your life influences others. If you are a parent with children or if you are a child with older parents, your life influences their way of life. Whether you are an employer or an employee, your relationship with those above you, below you, and beside you influences them. If you are not a natural leader, you will still want to be your best at home, in the community, or at work. Thus, you will pick up something to read that will help you.

Regretfully, most materials on leadership emphasize the qualities seen in natural leadership. Few ever highlight what it takes to be a spiritual leader. There is a difference. In his book *Spiritual Leadership*, J. Oswald Sanders lists the qualities of natural and spiritual leadership side by side. There you see the difference.

Natural Leadership	Spiritual Leadership
Self-confident	Confident in God
Knows men	Also knows God
Makes own decisions	Seeks God's will
Ambitious	Humble
Creates methods	Follows God's example
Enjoys command	Delights in obedience to God
Independent	Depends on God[6]

When you compare Sanders's list to the lives of spiritual leaders in the Bible, you see that spiritual leadership is distinguished by two traits: the leader's character and cause.

A Different Character

A biblical example of a spiritual leader is David. He embodies all of Sanders's qualities listed above. Psalm 78:72 explains why. It says of David, "So he shepherded them according to the integrity of his heart, and guided them by the skillfulness of his hands."

Spiritual leadership begins with the integrity of your heart, for your heart directly affects the way (skillfulness) in which you lead.

David's leadership of Israel created a dynasty that would last for approximately 425 years. Few dynasties in the world have equaled the records of David's family. Though David made his mistakes, his heart was soft to God. Looking at David's life you realize that it was the integrity of his heart that made him effective as a leader.

David's integrity is seen in his relationship with others. He held a lasting friendship with Jonathan and an unchallenged loyalty with his inner circle of leaders called his "mighty men." Another mark of his integrity was the way he received and responded to criticism. David allowed Shimei, a member of King Saul's clan, to curse him, and he listened to Nathan the prophet when Nathan charged him with sinning with Bathsheba. David's integrity also surfaced in the way he handled his mistakes. When Nathan confronted him about Bathsheba, David admitted he had blown it. He asked

God for forgiveness. And he endured the painful consequences of his sin with godliness.

Though they may not say it out loud, those around you want you to be a spiritual leader. They want you to live and lead with integrity. When 1,300 senior executives were asked what traits were responsible for enhancing effectiveness, 71 percent placed integrity at the top of their list. Sadly though, another survey revealed that 45 percent of workers did not trust top management and 33 percent distrusted their immediate bosses.[7] Make no mistake. Your family depends on you to be a spiritual leader as well. While majoring in psychology at Oklahoma State University, I read a lot of case studies. One image in particular stayed with me. It was the picture of a grown man kicking a beach ball across a room. In this study, the parents were allowed to enter a playroom and play with the toys. With their children watching from another room, some parents were respectful of the toys and others were not. Before each child could enter the room, they were told what they could and could not do with the toys. However, when released into the room, each child did exactly what they saw their parents do. In their mind, if it was right for their parents, it was right for them. Their parents had set the bar for conduct and character.

That is why it is important that you not forget that spiritual leadership is not a way to work. It is a way of life. It is who you are. And who you are directly affects what you do and the way you do it, which ultimately affects everyone around you. That is why, whether they say it or not, all around you want you to be a spiritual leader.

A Different Cause

Another distinguishing factor of a spiritual leader is that he or she gives himself or herself to a cause, not an end. There is a difference. This concept may be hard to grasp, for often we confuse an end with a cause. Former Washington Redskins football coach and now NASCAR race team owner Joe Gibbs alludes to this in his book *Racing to Win*. Gibbs states:

> The world sells us a bill of goods. Society says that a person cannot be successful without making money and gaining position, prestige, or power—or in my case, winning football games and, now, auto races. If you fall for the world's line, you will scratch and claw your way through life, trying to accomplish the goals and gather the trophies that the world values, only to discover too late that the most important matters of life lie elsewhere—in your relationship with God, your family, and the people around you.[8]

Money, position, prestige, power, and winning football games and auto races are all ends. Yet Gibbs says what is most important is a cause.

Seeing and pointing toward a cause can be hard in life because we find it challenging to tell the difference between an end and a cause. It helps if you can compare the distinguishing features of both.

An End	A Cause
Fills a want	Fills a need
Benefits a few	Benefits all
Does something good	Establishes what is right
Makes the moment better	Makes life better
Rewards achievement	Rewards effort
May add to the pockets	Will add to the person
Considers the now	Looks down the road
Pleases yourself or others	Pleases God

When you look at spiritual leaders in Scripture, you will see they understood the difference between an end and a cause. They knew that living and leading by a cause means giving yourself to something that is bigger than you, that benefits more than you, and points all attention to someone greater than you.

In their book *On Mission with God*, Avery Willis and Henry Blackaby identify seven spiritual leaders who lived and led for a cause.[9]

The Individual	Their Cause
Abraham	To be a blessing for all peoples
Moses	To help Israel become a blessing for all peoples
David	To establish a kingdom without end
Jesus	To be the savior for all peoples
Peter	To establish a church for all peoples
Paul	To present the gospel for all peoples
John	To lead all peoples to worship God

If you want to test and see if you are living for an end instead of a cause, use 1 Corinthians 10:31 to evaluate your passions and actions. It states, "Therefore, whether you eat or drink, or whatever you do, do all to the glory of God." Remember, living and leading for a cause will involve giving yourself to something bigger than you, to benefit more than you, and to give attention to someone greater than you. You know you are living and leading for a cause when the aim of all you do is to reveal to all the greatness of God.

In short, if you want to know if you are being a spiritual leader, stop and picture your heart. Just as the heart is the muscle that drives the body, the heart of the leader is the muscle that drives your leadership. Therefore just as your physical heart has four chambers that must work, your heart as a spiritual leader has two components that must function. First is leading from your character. Your character will determine the depth and quality of your influence. The second component is leading toward a cause. Who you are determines what you do. Your strength of character will determine your focus toward and passion for a godly cause. When you are leading from your character (godly integrity) toward a cause (it is bigger than you for God's glory), then you know you are living and leading as a spiritual leader.

Spiritual Leadership ... Stretches You

Because spiritual leadership involves you in matters bigger than you for someone greater than you, you often find yourself in situations that painfully stretch you. Picture Moses, for example. When God charged him from the burning bush to lead Israel out of Egypt, Moses told God, "I can't." In fact, Moses listed all the reasons why he could not. Yet it was not that Moses had never led before. You might remember that Moses was raised by Pharaoh's daughter and was well trained. Like other children of royalty, he attended the school of the pharaohs. The Jewish historian Josephus records that as a young man it was Moses who led the Egyptian forces to overtake the Ethiopians in battle (*Jewish Antiquities* 2.243–51). He had more leadership experience than most. Yet when God asked him to lead Israel's exodus, he felt inadequate for the task. He felt inadequate because spiritual leadership will always require more of you than natural leadership. Spiritual leadership will stretch you like no other form of leadership.

You may recall that although Moses had been successful in Egypt, he had also killed a man and fled to the wilderness. For forty years, Moses lived as a fugitive tending sheep instead of leading people. Then God told Moses He wanted to use him to lead His people to the promised land. As most of us would do, Moses pushed back from the cause feeling inadequate for the task.

You have probably given God the same push back for the same reasons as Moses. Yet Henry Blackaby insightfully says when you look throughout the Bible, "God doesn't call the equipped. He equips the called."[10] You will always feel ill equipped for the causes of God. You will always feel as though you have made too many mistakes for God to use you as a spiritual leader, but remember Moses.

Spiritual leadership will lead you to accept a cause beyond your experience, which makes us feel uncomfortable. Furthermore, it will require you to live and lead with integrity, which in many cases is not only uncommon, it can be unpopular. So like Moses, there will be times when you will want to push away from spiritual leadership. But do not lose heart. God knows that spiritual leadership is hard. He knows it will stretch you. That is why God always has a special relationship with those willing to live and lead as spiritual leaders.

God Encourages You

A great example of the special relationship God has with spiritual leaders is recorded in Haggai 2:20–23. Persian ruler Darius I made Zerubbabel governor in 538 BC. Zerubbabel's first act as a leader was to rebuild the temple of God. They raised money immediately and began the work. All was well and Zerubbabel was applauded for his leadership. However, Persia removed its financial aid to Jerusalem and the work of rebuilding the temple stopped. After fifteen years of struggling, Haggai's voice rallied the people to return to complete the temple. As the people became eager, their leader needed encouragement. He struggled with this for fifteen years. He probably wondered if there were more important needs than this. Where would the resources come from? What would happen if they failed again? Haggai's statement to Zerubbabel in Haggai 2:20–23 is an encouraging word every leader needs to hear. Zerubbabel is reminded that God takes and makes leaders.

Oftentimes the circumstances in life blind you to the truth that God handpicks you for the responsibilities He gives you. After the terrorist attack on the World Trade Center on September 11, 2001, President George W. Bush called James Merritt, then president of the

Southern Baptist Convention, along with other religious leaders to the White House. In an Oval Office meeting with a handful of these leaders, President Bush asked their opinion of the situation. Merritt remained silent, until the president asked his opinion. Merritt responded, "Mr. President, as fellow believers, we believe in the sovereignty of God. God knew that this was going to happen and it was God's plan for you to be our president at this time. You are God's man for this hour."[11]

Over the years I have talked with leaders at various levels. It does not matter if they were governors, agency presidents, or parents concerned about their families. All leaders, at one time or another, feel inadequate to the task. Yet if you are trying to fulfill God's cause with godly character, you need to acknowledge the following: of all the people in the world God could have chosen to carry out your responsibilities, an all-knowing God handpicked you. He knows you can do it. Trust Him.

Though it may be worded differently in verse 23, this was the message God gave to Zerubbabel to encourage him. It is the same encouragement God gives you when you feel stretched as a spiritual leader. God says, "Don't worry. I will take you and make you my spiritual leader."

God Takes You

Some might think that saying "An all-knowing God has handpicked you for the roles and responsibilities you have" sounds like a pep talk from a motivational speaker. Well, it is. However, the motivational speaker is God. In Haggai 2:23, God uses his prophet Haggai to tell a discouraged Zerubbabel, "'In that day,' says the LORD of hosts, 'I will take you, Zerubbabel My servant, the son of Shealtiel,' says the LORD, 'and will make you like a signet ring; for I have chosen you,' says the LORD of hosts."

The Hebrew word *take* (laqakh) used in this verse literally means to take firmly by the hand. Three times in Genesis it is used figuratively for taking a wife in marriage (Gen. 4:19; 6:2; 11:29). What a great image from God. When you strive to live and lead as a spiritual leader, God takes you by the hand and assumes a partnering relationship with you. He will lead you as you lead others in His character for His cause. Furthermore, this puts you in esteemed company. The Bible records the following leaders who were also taken by God.

- Abraham: as the father of God's chosen people (Josh. 24:3)
- The nation of Israel: to be His people and He their God (Deut. 4:20)
- Levites: to serve God in the sanctuary (Num. 18:1–7)
- David: to be God's prince over Israel (2 Sam. 7:8)
- Amos: to represent God in Bethel (Amos 7:15)

Yet before you form a sense of superiority, look at what God expects His spiritual leaders to do when He takes them. He told Zerubbabel in Haggai 2:23 (NIV), "I will take you, my servant Zerubbabel son of Shealtiel." As his leader, God takes you and expects you to be a servant. He expects you to serve.

In the King James Version of the Bible, the word *leader* appears 3 times, while the word *servant* appears 489 times. You might think that this is because leadership was not a hot topic when the King James Version was translated. That may be true, for when the New International Version was translated, the word *leader* had increased to appear 79 times. However, the word *servant* had also increased to 515 times.

No matter which translation you read, it is clear that when God gives you responsibilities requiring spiritual leadership, He expects you to lead as He did—as a servant. Yet being a servant-leader does not come easily. That is why God also makes the leaders that He takes.

God Makes You

God made a commitment to Zerubbabel that as his leader, God would make him His signet ring. During the sixth century BC, a signet ring was an owner's prized possession. It represented the owner by bearing his personal insignia and was used to authorize letters and documents. It was so special to the owner that he wore it either around his neck or on his right hand.

God's promise to Zerubbabel is His promise to you. God will make you the leader He needs you to be by keeping you close to Him. Through your closeness to God, you will bear His insignia. In time you will bear His likeness. Through your closeness to God He will authorize His work through you. You will bear fruit, fruit that lasts (John 15:5). God will make you the leader He needs you to be by offering to keep you around His neck and on His right hand. God will make you a spiritual leader if you will take full advantage of your special relationship with Him.

In his book *Making the Most of Life*, J. R. Miller writes about the famous Renaissance artist Leonardo da Vinci. As a student, Leonardo was unaware of the depths of his talents. But his teacher saw them. In order to bring his gifts to the surface, Leonardo's old and talented teacher began a painting. Before completing the work, he handed the brush to Leonardo and told him to finish it. Fearful at first, Leonardo refused. Yet at the insistence of his teacher, Leonardo took the brush and began to paint. His first strokes were timid, calculated, and stiff. Slowly his creativity took over and what his teacher had seen in him surfaced before his eyes. Upon finishing the work, Leonardo called for his teacher to view his work. Overjoyed with what his young student had become, the old teacher embraced his student and said, "My son, I paint no more."[12]

Like the old teacher, God sees in you what you do not. Like the old teacher, God offers a special working relationship with you to bring out what you do not see. Many times that means God taking you and handing you a responsibility of spiritual leadership that will make you uncomfortable. It will painfully stretch you. But as you finish the work God entrusted to you, He surfaces from you a confidence and creativity in spiritual leadership you had not seen before. He will make you the leader He sees in you, the spiritual leader you need to be. However, this will not happen if you do not take the brush of opportunity and keep a close relationship with God as your teacher.

Spiritual Leadership ... Targets You

When you begin to realize all you are and all that you can do with God as a spiritual leader, life is good. You are amazed at what you are able to accomplish with God. That is when you start receiving extra attention. Yes, there will be those who see what you are doing and the godly way you are doing it and will want to join you. However, the attention I am talking about is adversarial. You will begin receiving special attention from the one who wants to stop you and your work—Satan himself. And when Satan gets his eye on you, you can expect him to attack.

In John 10:10, Jesus reveals His desire for your life. Referring to his followers, Jesus professes, "I have come that they may have life, and that they may have it more abundantly." In that same verse Jesus exposes Satan's aim for your life. Calling Satan a thief, Jesus says, "The thief does not come except to steal, and to kill, and to destroy." Satan's aim is to destroy. His initial desire is to destroy any opportunity you have for surrendering your life to Jesus. If that fails, then his aim is to destroy your effectiveness as a spiritual leader with Jesus. Make no mistake. When you live and lead as a spiritual leader, you become the target of spiritual attacks.

Targeting You Early

In Matthew 4:1–11, Jesus had just been baptized by John the Baptist. Many believe that Jesus' baptism marks the beginning of his earthly ministry. That is why I do not think it is a coincidence that Satan tempts Jesus right after His baptism. Satan wants to destroy God's cause through Jesus before He can really begin fulfilling it.

One of my greatest heartaches as a pastor is seeing unrealized potential in God's people. Statistics show that most salvation experiences occur in individuals under the age of eighteen. However, when they turn eighteen and go to college, only a small percentage continue their walk with God once they emerge from college. At a point when God could really use them to advance His cause, Satan has somehow gotten to them and is destroying God's opportunity of fulfilling His cause through them.

Satan's Tactics

Destroying God's opportunity of fulfilling his cause was Satan's strategy with Jesus. Matthew 4:1–11 even reveals the tactics he used then and still uses today. Satan first tempted Jesus to turn stones into bread. Because of fasting, Jesus was hungry. Thus, Satan tempted Him to turn stones into bread and eat. It was simple enough. Jesus had an important need and Satan gave Him an immediate opportunity to satisfy it.

Satan distracts many from God's cause by confusing what is important with what is immediate. Jesus had a real need and having bread in hand would have satisfied it. Though the bread was an immediate need it was not the most important need. Jesus' most important need was developing his strength in and devotion to God. That was the purpose behind his fast. With a simple act of distraction—meeting an immediate need instead of staying focused on what was most important—Satan would have developed a habit in Jesus that would ultimately have destroyed God's cause through Him.

Satan uses the same tactics today. Satisfying the immediate instead of focusing on the important is one of the main challenges to spiritual leadership. There will always be one more communication to make, one more task to finish, one more need to meet, and one more expectation to fulfill before getting to what God deems important. Often we even let someone else's emergency become our urgency. In doing so, we have once again let the immediate overshadow the important. Fulfilling God's cause is put on the back burner, while we try to fix or fulfill everything else.

Satan also uses power and ambition to distract us from God's cause. He told Jesus to realize his God-given abilities and throw Himself down from a tower. Jesus and others would see God's promise fulfilled as angels would catch Him and protect Him from harm. Also, Satan offered Jesus all the kingdoms of the world if Jesus would bow down and worship him. Again, Jesus knew they would all be under His rule eventually. However, a simple bow to Satan would expedite everything.

If your college graduation was like mine, it seemed we were all eager to exert our abilities and fulfill our ambitions as quickly as possible. Yet as most of us can now attest, one ambition is readily replaced by another and none of them is quickly satisfied. That means you are now living in the endless cycle of always using your strength to fulfill your ambitions. And God? Well, you have placed God somewhere on the sidelines of your life.

He is there to mainly cheer you on as you try to win your own game. Somewhere, somehow, your life with God subtly changed. It has become all about what you can do in your strength instead of seeing God's cause for your life and fulfilling it in His strength.

A Focused Defense

Though Satan's attacks have proved to be effective, you can withstand them. Jesus did and so have many others. All that is required is a disciplined effort of staying focused.

Often we let other items replace God's cause. There will always be fires to put out in life. Satan will always generate various obstacles against God's cause. Sometimes, however, we allow the obstacles to become our objective. We become so focused on overcoming the obstacles that we lose sight of the cause. In doing so, we have become nothing more than fixers when God desires to use us as fulfillers of His cause.

We even let our agendas or the agendas of others replace God's cause. After Jesus had performed several miracles in Galilee, his brothers told Jesus He needed to go to Jerusalem so more could see what He was doing. Scripture records that although his brothers gave Him this advice, they still did not believe in Him. Jesus stayed focused on God's cause and God's timing and told His brothers in John 7:6 (NIV) "The right time for me has not yet come; for you any time is right."

Satan will use challenging obstacles and competing agendas to distract you from God's cause for your life.

That is why Scripture records how Jesus was able to stay focused in spite of all of Satan's constant attempts to distract Him. In Mark 1:35–38, the Bible states,

> [35] Now in the morning, having risen a long while before daylight, He went out and departed to a solitary place; and there He prayed. [36] And Simon and those who were with Him searched for Him. [37] When they found Him, they said to Him, "Everyone is looking for You." [38] But He said to them, "Let us go into the next towns, that I may preach there also, because for this purpose I have come forth."

Even Jesus made time to be alone with God. He knew if he didn't focus on God first, life and others would have him focusing on everything else. He emerged from his time with God focused and confident of God's purpose for his life and for that day. Think of it. If Jesus needed time alone with God each day to stay focused, how much more do you and I need that time with God?

Spiritual Leadership ... Makes a Difference

Earlier you read what makes spiritual leadership different from natural leadership. God summarizes the difference in 2 Samuel 23:4. Referring to spiritual leaders, God writes, "And he shall be like the light of the morning when the sun rises, a morning without clouds, like the tender grass springing out of the earth, by clear shining after rain."

God says you will know a spiritual leader when you see one. She or he will be as clear and moving as a sunrise on a cloudless day. However, God also explains that spiritual leaders are not individuals who just look different. Just as the sun that rises causes the grass to grow, spiritual leaders make a difference.

Over the years I have met men and women I would classify as spiritual leaders. Some were ministers. Many were not. Some you would recognize if I gave you their names. Most of them, you would not. Name recognition does not make you more or less of a spiritual leader. All that matters is your willingness to fulfill God's cause with a godly character. That means being willing to go through the painful moments when God stretches you, and overcoming the many times Satan attacks you. It means that when you come to the end of your life, your Lord and others can say that you made a difference.

Part Two
Caring for God's People

Prayer Care
Kip Wahlquist

One of my favorite passages in the Bible is Mark 2:1–12 where we read the account of Jesus healing the paralytic.

> [1] And again He entered Capernaum after some days, and it was heard that He was in the house. [2] Immediately many gathered together, so that there was no longer room to receive them, not even near the door. And He preached the word to them. [3] Then they came to Him, bringing a paralytic who was carried by four men. [4] And when they could not come near Him because of the crowd, they uncovered the roof where He was. So when they had broken through, they let down the bed on which the paralytic was lying. [5] When Jesus saw their faith, He said to the paralytic, "Son, your sins are forgiven you." [6] And some of the scribes were sitting there and reasoning in their hearts, [7] "Why does this Man speak blasphemies like this? Who can forgive sins but God alone?" [8] But immediately, when Jesus perceived in His spirit that they reasoned thus within themselves, He said to them, "Why do you reason about these things in your hearts? [9] Which is easier, to say to the paralytic, 'Your

sins are forgiven you,' or to say, 'Arise, take up your bed and walk'? [10] But that you may know that the Son of Man has power on earth to forgive sins"—He said to the paralytic, [11] "I say to you, arise, take up your bed, and go to your house." [12] Immediately he arose, took up the bed, and went out in the presence of them all, so that all were amazed and glorified God, saying, "We never saw anything like this!"

It has been said that people do not really care about how much you know until they know how much you care. In the above text we clearly observe the compassionate action of the bearers of the paralytic. They were willing to do whatever it took to get the paralytic man close to Jesus because the news was spreading: demons were being driven out; fevers were being healed; diseases—even leprosy—were being cured. The care we see demonstrated was laborious. Picture four men carrying a physically impaired man on a mat of some type, trying to get close to Jesus, the healer. Who were these men? Were they friends? Family? Business associates? Neighbors? We do not know for sure, but whoever they were, they cared enough to bring the needy one to Jesus. The crowds in Capernaum were too thick for them to accomplish their mission. Determined as they were and not willing to let the wall of people prevent them from helping the needy one, they chose the high road: literally, the roof.

Again, imagine climbing a wall, holding tightly to your corner of the mat, struggling not to spill your living cargo, and making your way up a ladder and over to a spot on the roof under which Jesus would, you hoped, be found. After catching your breath, you might find yourself praying, "Please don't move, Jesus." These guys were serious. The needy one was going to see Jesus today. Oh, and there was just one more step to accomplish: the needy one needed to be lowered through the roof in order to get near Jesus. No problem. Dig a hole through the roof. Lower the needy one down with the rope securely attached to the mat. Try not to hit Jesus in the head with the needy one. And then wait to see what will happen next. These four men exemplified caring action to help the needy one get close to the Healer. The results were immediate and spectacular.

So, you may be asking, "What does the healing of the paralytic have to do with prayer care?" Like the care demonstrated by the four helpers in Mark 2, prayer care is compassionate love in action that takes effort and intentionality. Prayer care is caring enough to pray for the needs of the hurting and bringing him or her into the presence of Jesus. It may be a brief prayer or it may last for several minutes. It may be a one-time prayer or it may be many prayers laboriously stretched out for months or even years. Regardless of their duration or frequency, your prayers for people in need matter. James 5:16*b* reminds us of this fact: "The effective, fervent prayer of a righteous man avails much."

When I am ministering to a person in need, I often wonder if he or she has experienced someone in recent memory gently place a hand on his or her shoulder and invite God's presence to fill and touch him or her with His love and grace. What a privilege it is to help carry the person's mat into the presence of the Lord, and then observe His Philippians 4:7 peace as it touches the person's life as the burdens and needs of the hour are laid at Jesus' feet.

It is my custom to open or close a caring ministry contact with prayer, and at times when I have forgotten or have been too rushed, I have heard from the ministry receiver, who was accustomed to this tradition, that she or he really missed the prayer time. One person reported that she found it to be just as important as, if not more important than, any words we may have shared together.

One unfortunately all-too-common missed prayer care opportunity involves the expression "I'll pray for you." Though well intentioned and heartfelt, this caring promise is not always kept. At times I have forgotten to pray for needs and time-sensitive matters even though I had said I would. So I have learned through the school of hard knocks that one solution to my humanness is to pray for the situation immediately. Occasionally, I will ask the person if I can pray for him or her right then. I have yet to have anyone, believer or nonbeliever, turn me down. We might be on the phone, in the car, walking somewhere, at work, at school, watching a sporting event. The location does not matter, though discretion is advised. It is vital that you follow through. It blesses my pastoral heart, as I know it does God's, to see people coming together with support and love, wherever they may be on the highways and byways of life, caring for one another by the intentional ministry of prayer care.

If you are leading a small group or class, be sure that prayer care is a priority in your group time together. If you are discipling or mentoring someone, be sure that you are praying for her or him in the person's presence. If you are leading a ministry team, be sure that you know your team and are taking time to pray for one another's needs and concerns as you go through life together. If you are supervising volunteers, let them know you are praying for them, and ask for prayer requests and praise reports from time to time to demonstrate you truly do care. A brief e-mail or card sent just to say that she or he came to mind today and you prayed for her or him can be wonderful encouragement. Have you made it easy for people in your church to request prayer through a telephone hotline, Web site or e-mail form, or handwritten card that can be placed in the offering plate? These administrative systems can assist your church in being more effective in the ministry of prayer care.

One obstacle I have frequently observed in the ministry of prayer care is that people believe they do not know how to pray well and therefore are feeling too intimidated or discouraged to act. My response has been twofold: one, use the prayers already recorded in the Bible to guide you, and two, rely on the Holy Spirit who can lead you (see Rom. 8:26–27).

For example, the apostle Paul's prayers recorded in Ephesians 1:15–23 and 3:14–21 and in Colossians 1:9–14 can be prayed verbatim or are very helpful templates that can be adapted to fit a person's current needs. Praying the Psalms is another use of the biblical text if one does not know how to pray for a specific situation. Consider using Psalm 46 for the person who is facing a trial and needs to be reminded of God's power and presence. Praying David's penitential Psalm 51 is helpful for the hurting person who has confessed his or her sin and is feeling shame and guilt. People who have been wronged can especially relate to Psalms 55 and 56 in light of their suffering and struggles with hurt, anger, and a yearning for justice. For people who are feeling fear or are being threatened, Psalm 63 provides a helpful prayer template. If a ministry receiver is complaining about the offenses of the sinful people in her or his life, prayer care can be found in Psalm 64. You get the idea—use the Psalms as a prayer book as you pray for the hurting.

When you are completely dependent on the Holy Spirit in the ministry of prayer care you will be praying according to God's will. In Matthew 10:19–20, Jesus instructed the twelve disciples about how to respond when they get arrested: "But when they deliver you up, do not worry about how or what you should speak. For it will be given to you in that hour what you should speak; for it is not you who speak, but the Spirit of your Father who speaks in you."

You can be confident in the work of the Holy Spirit to speak through you in any prayer care situation as you trust in His filling and supernatural power. Even in moments of silence when you do not know how to pray, remember, "He makes intercession for the saints according to the will of God" (Rom. 8:27).

One of the highlights of my week is to witness a ministry receiver experience the healing presence and power of God in the prayer moment by hearing God's voice, not just mine. After taking a few minutes to listen to the person's situation, you can facilitate this divine moment by simply asking God what He wants to reveal or say to the ministry receiver about the situation at hand, and then remain quiet. In this posture of being still and knowing that He is God (see Ps. 46:10), God may choose to manifest His timeless presence and speak to the heart with His still, soft voice. Time and time again I have seen people released from fear, doubt, confusion, pain, shame, guilt, and lies that have kept them in spiritual and emotional bondage. In this manner of prayer care, God can transform a life right before your eyes through the resurrection power of His Holy Spirit, and the ministry receiver is forever changed because you did what you could to bring the person into the presence of Jesus through the ministry of prayer care.

Do you know someone who is in need? Might there be a corner of the person's mat that you can help carry in prayer to bring him or her one step closer to Jesus? Your availability to pray is your greatest ability. Help the hurting around you to get near the Healer, to access His comfort, to receive His extra measure of grace. Remember, Jesus is responsible for the results. He knows this person's needs better than you do. God and God alone is the cure giver. He will answer in His perfect timing and in His tailor-made ways. Your prayer care can and does make an eternal difference.

Investing for Impact
Steve Hopkins

Let me remind you about the story of Joe, just an average guy, moved from his island home to the big city who got involved in a church. Before long, Joe gained the reputation of being an encourager and a sacrificial, generous giver. He was respected, but still average. Then things changed for Joe, and his journey from average to extraordinary began.

Joe's story started to get interesting when a new believer tried to join the church, a man with a background that caused everyone to be cautious. Everyone, that is, but Joe. He witnessed how the Father worked in this new believer and decided to take a chance. Joe walked that novice right into the leadership team meeting, sharing with them the evidence of the Father's hand, evidence that demanded a hearing.

Joe did not stop there. The church sent him to encourage a new congregation. Determined to invest in the new believer, Joe brought him to the new church plant to join him as apprentice. When time came for the new church to sponsor a mission trip, Joe took his apprentice-turned-journeyman with him. The two added a protégé, and, no exaggeration, they changed their world.

You may have already recognized average Joe—better known as Barnabas (Acts 4:36–37). When you track the influence of Barnabas, it is off the charts. While mentoring Paul and John Mark (11:22–25; 12:25), he led his team to establish new churches, defining the role of missions and missionaries (Acts 13:1–5). His background as a Levite from Cyprus equipped him to go to the Gentile world with the gospel. Adding together the thirteen letters of Paul, the Gospel Mark recorded, and the influence of Mark's Gospel on Matthew and Luke, Barnabas influenced 60 percent of the New Testament.

Bible scholar and author Howard Hendricks writes:

> So while we rightly think of Paul as the strategic spokesman for Christ in the New Testament, we must never forget that behind Paul there was a Barnabas. In fact, Paul seemed to be echoing Barnabas when he wrote to Timothy, "The things you have heard me say in the presence of many witnesses entrust to reliable men who will also be qualified to teach others. (2 Timothy 2:2)"[13]

I like this comparison by Bobby Clinton and Laura Raab:

> Barnabas is a most underrated contributor to the spread of New Testament Christianity. In today's modern athletic world, he would be one of those unsung linemen who renegotiates his contract upward to a multi-year multi-million-dollar one. And he would deserve it.[14]

What is keeping you from a legacy of influence like that of Barnabas? Do you have an investment strategy?

While *coaching* and *mentoring* have become buzzwords today, often the "average Joe" and "average Jane" cannot envision their name tag reading "Coach" or "Mentor." Perhaps the idea of investment would free us to start. Like the investment broker's dramatic illustrations of compound interest, we must see the long-term value of investing in the lives of those around us.

Definition

Robert Clinton and Paul Stanley define mentoring as "a relational experience in which one person empowers another by sharing God-given resources."[15] Our God-given resources—knowledge, wisdom, skills, experiences, opportunities—are meant to be shared. Failure to invest exposes self-centered selfish living. Hoarding all the Father has given produces a person like the unfaithful servant who fails to invest his talent (Matt. 25:24–30), or the vine that fails to produce fruit (John 15:2). As a follower of Christ, you must invest in others. Whatever you have learned from Him, you can pass on to others, if you are willing to share.

The goal is not to clone the mentor, but to help others grow toward their potential. The Father has a unique plan for each believer, and His agenda supersedes the mentor's agenda. Although important, content should not be the focus. Curriculum may be used, but the investment should not be curriculum driven. The Father's work in their lives should emerge as the game plan. Our desire is to see them following the Leader, not us. The ultimate goal: their faith will rest not on men's wisdom, but on God's power (1 Cor. 2:5; see also 1 Cor. 11:1).

Our investment can happen in many ways. It does not have to be highly structured, but it does need to be intentional. The relationship can be formal or informal, scheduled or sporadic. The exchange can take place over a long time or just once. Often it will be face-to-face, but it may happen over a long distance. Investment may be as simple as linking a person with important resources: relationships, contacts, networks, opportunities, methods, experiences, information, and skills. Investment can also come by modeling habits and disciplines that help them take the next step in their walk with Christ. Insights learned, discernment developed, character issues refined, and perspectives gained through life experiences—all expand your investment. These simple relational deposits are worth more than gold.

Investment requires involvement. At times, you will need to walk in the trenches alongside others, and it will get messy. It may even hurt. Loving the way Jesus loved demands we get into their world. A verse that has challenged me for years is John 15:12: "This is My commandment, that you love one another *as I have loved you*" (emphasis added). Had Jesus stopped with "love one another," it would be much easier. However, He added five words, "as I have loved you," forever raising the bar on what it means to love. Jesus defined biblical love: He left His world, heaven, and came to my world, earth, and sacrificially gave Himself away to meet my greatest need, forgiveness of sins, that I might have a relationship with the Father. Jesus gave the criteria by which people will identify us: "A new commandment I give to you, that you love one another; *as I have loved you*, that you also love one another. By this all will know that you are My disciples, if you have love for one another" (John 13:34–35, emphasis added).

Misconceptions

Misconceptions can sabotage our efforts to invest in others.[16] The most common misconception is that the investor must be a wise old person with all the answers to all the questions. We need multiple mentors, with different life experiences, who can help with specific growth areas of our life. We must not expect one person to be our guru for all of life, and we must never present ourselves to another as such. Age is not nearly as important as experience. Having problems with your smartphone? Find a sixteen-year-old to mentor you. When we let go of the misconception of there being one person who has the answer, we discover there are scores of people who could benefit from our life experience and insight.

A sibling to the first misconception can be our feeling that we are not qualified to invest in another. If you are learning and growing in your relationship with Christ and are willing to share what you are learning, you qualify. Again, you are not required to have all the answers, to be the perfect model, or to hold the key for a dramatic breakthrough. Claiming to be unqualified can be an expression of pride, believing it is really about you and what you have to offer. Never underestimate the work of the Father in your life and His ability to multiply the loaves and fishes when placed in His hands.

A third common misconception causes us to doubt the value of merely spending time with another. In reality, each mundane moment you spend with someone can create incremental value, building a meaningful influence over time. Gary Mayes suggests, "The remarkable impact of mentoring is not in the drama of a single moment, but in the cumulative impact of one person sharing their life and their experience with another over time."[17] Mentoring changes lives by consistently investing, even in small amounts.

Strategy

To start developing your own investment strategy, first look at the possibilities around you. Take a piece of paper and ask the Father to bring to mind the people who cross your path on a regular basis. Family, friends, coworkers, a new member in your Sunday school class or small group, the person who suggested in passing you get together for coffee—there is little risk in getting their names down and beginning to pray. Then look for opportunities to establish a relationship; it all starts with relationship. Sometimes an investment relationship just happens naturally. Others require efforts that are more deliberate. You do not have to become best friends to invest in someone, but you do need a relationship. Do not do ministry alone; take someone with you. See every ministry opportunity as a mentoring opportunity.

Next, determine the need, and consider what you have to offer. Approach the relationship with the attitude "I am here to help, and I will do what I can." Do not force it. When you live a Romans 12 life—surrendered, authentic, humble, loving, diligent, and so on—and make yourself available, there will be no shortage of opportunities. If you take on the mind of Christ, looking out not for your interests, but for the interests of others (Phil 2:1–5), there will be no need to take out an ad for protégés. More than likely, your most difficult decisions will concern the limitations of time and energy.

If the relationship becomes more formal, such as a mentoring or coaching opportunity, clearly define expectations. When appropriate, you need to address questions about how regularly you will meet, how accountable each will be to the other, what communication channels you will use, the level of confidentiality you will observe, and how you will know closure has been achieved need to be addressed.[18] Six-month time commitments give you both an opportunity to opt out or re-up. Guidelines are very helpful in establishing the relationship, but do not let the relational aspects be hampered by unnecessary formality.

One of the best ways to develop as a mentor is to be mentored. Terry Walling recommends developing multiple mentors as part of his focused-living process.[19] We greatly enhance our development with a balance of mentoring relationships. Some will be mentors who are steps ahead of us in experience and knowledge. Others will be peers who can provide objective perspectives and help us think through situations. As we gain insights from those who invest in us, we are better equipped to share our lives with those the Father brings our way.

My experience with *MasterLife* became a significant spiritual marker in my life. Avery Willis challenged me with one simple plan: "one person is to disciple one or more until the one being discipled can disciple yet a third person. Then the two should win two others and disciple them, and so forth."[20] Following the plan, if every person would invest in another for six months, and if the first person would follow the model, the entire population of the world could be touched in a little more than sixteen years. It is not rocket science. We can change the world one life at a time.

Finally, never underestimate the importance of prayer. Pray for opportunities to invest your life, and trust the Father to open doors. Pray for those who are in your circle of influence, and watch to see how the Father is at work in their lives.

Challenge

People who played the supporting role, encouraging and investing in the lives of others, fill the pages of the Bible. We find Joseph, supporting Mary as she carried our Lord; Joanna and Susanna, supporting Jesus and the disciples; Stephanas, Fortunatus, and Achaicus, refreshing Paul's spirit. The list could go on and on, many whose names we may never know. The unnamed armor-bearer in 1 Samuel 14 provides an excellent example. God gave Jonathan a hill to take, but he needed help. After he shared his vision, his armor-bearer responded, "Do all that is in your heart. Go then; here I am with you, according to your heart" (v. 7). The result was the Lord saved Israel that day (v. 23).

Look around you. Is there a Paul who needs a Barnabas to get started, a Jonathan who needs an armor-bearer for the fight, an Esther who needs the courage of Mordecai? Can you imagine the joy in heaven for a tailor named J. D. Prevatt, who put his arm around a sixteen-year-old Billy Graham and shared the plan of salvation?[21] It is not a coincidence that you are where you are at any given moment. The Father has placed people in your circle of influence. With whom could you share your life? Today you can make an investment. Then watch for the returns, all for His glory.

Becoming the Lay Witness God Wants You to Be

David Wheeler

Nothing puts fear in the hearts of Christians quicker than the concept of evangelism. Even the most mature believers often find it difficult to share their faith. Over the years, this irrational fear has led to several unbiblical beliefs about the task of evangelism. So before we dive into various concepts and approaches to sharing Christ, let us first address some basic misconceptions about what evangelism is not.

Evangelism is not a choice. It is generally accepted in Christian circles that the majority of believers rarely shares their faith with another unsaved person. In fact, I have noticed this in my graduate-level evangelism classes. By a simple show of hands, on average well over half of the students will admit that they fall into this unfortunate category.

I am convinced that one of the contributing factors to the lack of evangelism is that it is taught as an individual choice rather than a biblical command. This is misleading and dangerous in reference to the Great Commission.

Consider what Jesus' says in Acts 1:8 (NIV), "But you will receive power when the Holy Spirit comes on you; and you will be my witnesses in Jerusalem, and in all Judea and Samaria, and to the ends of the earth." Note that the phrase "you will be my witnesses" is written as an imperative or better yet, as a direct command of Christ aimed at mobilizing His disciples into the world to fulfill His earlier promise as recorded in Mark 1:17 (NIV), "'Come, follow me,' Jesus said, 'and I will make you fishers of men.'"

Evangelism is not passing on information. There are hundreds of ways to effectively share Christ with an unbeliever. However, in doing so, one must remember that evangelism is not just sharing the right biblical information.

As I always tell my classes, "You cannot divorce Jesus' message from the man He represented." This simply means that Jesus not only shared the truth in word, He also embodied that same truth through a consistent lifestyle. While it is very important that one should be able to pass on the correct biblical knowledge relating to salvation, he or she must also validate that same knowledge to the world through the consistent testimony of a changed life.

Evangelism in not a spiritual gift. Contrary to popular belief in the church, evangelism is not listed as a spiritual gift in Scripture. Granted, while some people may have talents that aid in becoming more natural at evangelism, the call to evangelize is meant for the entire church. It is not reserved for a select few believers.

According to the Greek, the word *evangelism* is meant to be a noun (euangelion), not a verb (euangelizō) that means "to evangelize." The word for "evangelism" literally means "good news" or the "message." The problem is that most people define evangelism as sharing the good news (verb), when actually evangelism is the good news (noun). Our problem with evangelism is that we define it by the action, not the nature or essence of the action. At the core, evangelism is the "good news" of Christ and must be embraced as a lifestyle by every Christian.

Now that we know what evangelism is not, the remainder of this chapter will be dedicated to what evangelism is:

- evangelism is washing feet and sharing Christ
- learning the power of the towel and basin

Next to the Holy Spirit, the Bible, and the gospel message, there is nothing more powerful or useful in the call of evangelism than the towel and the basin. As demonstrated by Jesus in John 13, the example of washing the disciples' feet serves as a reminder of Christlike humility and surrender that should be manifested in the lives of all true believers. One thing is for sure: it is a life-changing concept in evangelism when put into daily practice.

While in college a young man began attending a weekly prayer group of which I was a member. When asked about his faith, he quickly responded that he was an agnostic in search of the truth.

After several weeks spent building a relationship, the young man was invited to stay after one of the meetings in order to discuss his questions related to Christianity. He seemed intrigued, and even stated that he wanted to "believe," but he "just couldn't see it." At that point, one of the coworkers in the prayer group stood up and quickly left the room, only to return a few minutes later with a couple of towels and a basin of water. After setting the basin at my feet, he then turned to the agnostic and said, "If you can't see what faith in Christ is all about, we will show you." He proceeded to wash my feet, allowing me to return the privilege. Afterward, we prayed and even sang a few worship songs. It was evident that the Holy Spirit was present.

The young man later explained that when he returned to his dorm room that evening, he was confused about what he believed and vowed never to return to the prayer group. However, all of this changed early the next morning. After lying in bed from midnight until about 3:30 a.m., desperately trying to forget what he had "seen and heard" (see Acts 4:18–20), all he could think about was Christ and especially the humble demonstration of washing feet. After hours of feeling God's conviction for sin and being unable to rest, he slipped to his knees and told Christ, "If you are there and if you are real as I saw and experienced tonight, I need you Lord Jesus to save me. I surrender everything. Please come into my life."

This former agnostic's life radically changed through the power of genuine faith as demonstrated through washing feet and proclaiming the saving message of Christ. For lack of a better description, we call this biblical approach "servanthood evangelism."

What Is Servanthood Evangelism?

Servanthood Evangelism Defined

Servanthood evangelism involves intentionally sharing Christ by modeling biblical servanthood. It is the simplest, most transferable, and yes, most fun approach for moving believers closer to a lifestyle marked by consistent witnessing. With all that said, servanthood evangelism is also the most biblical approach through intentionally demonstrating Christ's love and message to an unsaved world.

I should note that the aspect of intentionally connecting the verbal message of Christ through acts of service is what differentiates servanthood evangelism from the Social Gospel movement that became popular with liberal theologians over the past century. This movement does not verbally connect the message of Christ as savior to service.

Servanthood Evangelism Delivered

It is essential that Christians understand what kindness means, since it does not mean telling people what they want to hear so they will feel good about themselves. It also does not mean doing mere acts of kindness with no intended purpose toward evangelism. Granted, there are valuable ministries, such as taking a loaf of bread to newcomers, and others, which are helpful, though they are not explicitly evangelistic. Servanthood evangelism acknowledges this dilemma, and is by nature intentionally evangelistic.

Thirty years of ministerial experience reveals that servanthood evangelism leads to a full presentation of Christ much more often than if the concept of servanthood is ignored. This is especially true as evangelism relates to the lay minister. It all depends on the leadership of the Holy Spirit and the boldness of the witness who obediently verbalizes her or his faith.

So how can a layperson develop a lifestyle of evangelism marked by intentional service?

Learn to Identify Needs

The first step in developing an evangelistic lifestyle is learning how to identify the needs of the people. Police officers are trained to analyze situations immediately. If there is a problem or something suspicious, a good officer should be able to handle the situation in a professional and effective manner. Much in the same way, we as Christians need to train ourselves to spot the needs of hurting people.

Matthew 6:32–33 states plainly that while the unsaved spend their lives chasing after their own needs, Christians ought to first seek after the kingdom of God and His righteousness. In other words, as Christ followers, we must first be concerned with advancing God's kingdom and not our own. That means taking the focus from ourselves and aiming it toward those around us who are in desperate need of an encounter with Christ.

Jesus modeled this attitude in John 4 when He and His disciples traveled through Samaria (this went against Jewish religious tradition). Verse 4 (NIV) states that Jesus "had to go through Samaria." This was undoubtedly confusing for His disciples, because as good Jews they would never have intentionally traveled through Samaria. It is not until verse 7 and Jesus' encounter with the woman at the well that we are given a glimpse of why He chose to go against Jewish tradition. As the story progresses, it becomes obvious that His genuine concern for the woman's spiritual condition far outweighed His desire for adhering to religious traditions.

Go Where Needs Are

The next step in developing an evangelistic lifestyle is to go where the needs are. Returning to the example of Jesus in John 4, we can see that Jesus not only identified the needs of the people, but He went to them regardless of how it was perceived by others. As His followers, we need to have the same attitude when it comes to evangelism.

Christians must indentify needs and be willing to go where they exist, even if it means going into an unpleasant or unfamiliar setting. Too many Christians play it safe by avoiding hurting areas in favor of focusing their witnessing efforts on less abrasive and less challenging locations. This was not the approach of Christ.

Case in point: the woman at the well was not the type of person who would have been accepted by religious leaders in the Jerusalem temple. Not only was she an unclean Samaritan according to Jewish tradition, but she was an adulterous woman, maybe even a harlot. According to this view the woman would not have been deserving of Jesus' attention or God's grace. Samaritans were the offspring of Jews who had intermarried with people of other faiths and eventually mixed pagan traditions and teachings with the religion of Israel.

This makes the events of John 4 even more spectacular. While the disciples were disconnected from the woman's needs and appeared extremely uncomfortable, please note that this did not hinder Jesus and His desire to have an impact on the woman and the people of the surrounding community.

Initiate a Plan

The third step is to develop a life that is characterized by evangelism. When Jesus went to the woman at the well, He had a proven strategy. He listened to her politely, and spoke to her in a nonaggressive tone. Eventually, He confronted her with the truth without embarrassment or manipulation. Only then, when she was ready, did He offer the ultimate solution to her problem.

Once we identify the needs of people, we must initiate a plan to serve and meet that need. This is where the fun of servanthood evangelism comes into play. For example, let us say your neighbor's yard is full of leaves. According to the size of the job, the obvious response is to secure willing helpers from the church to assist in the servant opportunity. If you are sensitive and willing, hundreds of possibilities will soon arise.

This step centers on doing intentional acts of kindness for other people, simply because they are loved by God and made in His image. Is this not what Christ's sacrifice was all about? Did He not come to us while we were yet sinners, and die even for the ones who were hurling insults at Him while He hung on the cross?

Indeed, the incarnation of Jesus should be seen as the ultimate expression of servanthood evangelism. While He identified the world's need for forgiveness and a restored relationship with the Father, He didn't stop there. Jesus was willing to go where the need existed, namely to earth; and so He wrapped Himself in human flesh and came as one of us. He also initiated a plan to meet the desperate need of humanity, which was to die on the cross in our place in order to make restoration to the Father possible for all people. Lastly, He did not give up on us and leave us to our own devices to figure out how to live the Christian life. Christ sent "another," the Holy Spirit who is our comforter and sustainer. This leads us to the last step to developing a lifestyle of evangelism.

Be Willing to Stay

Once we initiate a plan to meet the needs of the people, we need to be willing to stay and invest our lives through servanthood. In John 4, after Jesus had ministered to the people from Sychar, He stayed with them for two days. Why is that? It seems logical that He stayed with them longer because He cared for them and wanted to develop lasting relationships.

This is exactly what we need to do as we try to develop lives that are characterized by evangelism and service. We need to be willing to forge relationships with people in our spheres of influence. They need to know that they are not just numbers, and that we are not simply marking off "evangelism" on our own personal list of things to do. Once this happens, people will realize that we care about them individually. This is one of the best illustrations of Christ's love for humanity.

Five Servanthood Evangelism Lay Projects That Work

1. Initiate a gas "buy-down." Secure a local gas station and buy down every gallon of gas that is sold from 11:00 a.m. to 1:00 p.m. by twenty-five cents per gallon, up to twenty gallons. For example, if gas is ordinarily $3.00 per gallon, it would be sold for $2.75 per gallon and the church would make up the difference. Church members would pump the gas and clean windshields.

2. Adopt local public schools. Take fresh donuts to the teachers' lounge each week. Or perhaps laypersons could volunteer to take up tickets for sporting events or feed the teachers for free on in-service days.

3. Contact neighborhood families. Laypersons could adopt their surrounding community by mapping out their neighborhood and praying for at least twenty unchurched families. Be encouraged to cook a meal or prepare a dessert for one or more of the families each week and utilize the delivery as an opportunity to ask for prayer requests and to get acquainted. Deliver the food in good dishes so that the family will have additional contact when they return them. One can also shovel snow, rake leaves, mow yards, or provide free babysitting. Acknowledging birthdays, graduations, and anniversaries can also be effective.

4. Adopt special days. For instance, give away chocolate on Valentine's Day or carnations on Mother's Day. Cookies work well throughout the year, especially at Christmas. As for Halloween, do reverse trick-or-treating by going out to neighbors and delivering small gifts of appreciation. Be on the lookout for servant projects at each of the houses you visit and be willing to offer assistance.

5. Use "intentional connection cards." The cards can say something as simple as "We just want you to know that we care." On the back might be a small map to the church and other pertinent information. The cards are good for any servant evangelism activity, but when utilized by Christians—in cases like anonymously paying someone's bill in a restaurant, or paying for the drive-through meal of the customers behind you—it is an effective way to plant seeds. For instance, a pastor in Richmond, Virginia, paid the check for the car behind him at a fast-food drive-through. He also tipped the worker and gave the person a connection card. When he returned to the same drive-through the next week, he was pleasantly surprised to find out that his act of service created a small movement. It seems that the next fourteen cars after him repeated

his kind deed and also paid the check for the car behind them.

Go to www.servantevangelism.com for more ideas. Never underestimate the power of servanthood.

Good Approaches to Sharing Your Faith

Prepare Your Personal Salvation Testimony

In today's culture, one's salvation testimony is essential because no one can argue with your experience. By using a simple outline you should be able to verbalize your salvation experience with anyone in no more than two minutes. Note the following outline:

1. My life before coming into a relationship with Christ.

2. How I came to personal faith in Christ.

3. How my life has changed since surrendering my life to Christ as my Lord and Savior.

Prepare Your Recovery Testimony

One's "recovery" testimony differs from a "salvation" testimony in that the purpose is to utilize one's life experiences in order to build a bridge to share the gospel. In short, it is putting empathy into action. For instance, suppose you have experienced the personal destruction of an addiction (alcohol, pornography, drugs, etc.), the pain of a divorce, or the loss of a loved one. In many cases, Satan will use the bitterness and bondage of these experiences to keep Christians from sharing about Christ. In reality, a "recovery" testimony provides the opportunity to brag on God's deliverance and to magnify the power of His gospel message. By possessing a sensitive spirit and a willingness to share one's story, the "recovery" testimony provides a natural transition into a presentation about the saving message of Christ. Note the following outline as you prepare your "recovery" testimony:

1. My life seemed normal until ...

2. I discovered hope and help in Jesus when ...

3. I am glad I have a personal relationship with Jesus today because ...

The transitional sentence from your testimony to the gospel message can be as simple as the statement "May I explain further how something like this can happen to you?" Believe it or not, in most cases the answer will be yes.

Use the "Romans Road"

This approach is one of the most basic and effective presentations of the gospel message. While it is suggested that you memorize the following verses, feel free to use your Bible. The outline goes as follows:

1. Take the person to Romans 3:23, "For all have sinned and fall short of the glory of God," in order to establish the concept of personal sin.

2. Take the person to Romans 6:23, "For the wages of sin *is* death, but the gift of God is

eternal life in Jesus Christ our Lord," in order
to establish the punishment and penalty for
sin ("death"). This also helps to introduce the
person to the grace and mercy of God ("eternal life"), which contrasts the eternal payment
("wages") of sin.

3. Take the person to Romans 5:8, "God demonstrates His own love toward us, in that while
we were still sinners, Christ died for us," to
further demonstrate God's mercy, grace, and
extraordinary love for His creation. Again,
this is in contrast to our natural state as sinners without hope for redemption.

4. Take the person to Romans 10:9–10, "If you
confess with your mouth the Lord Jesus and
believe in your heart that God has raised
Him from the dead, you will be saved. For
with the heart one believes unto righteousness, and with the mouth confession is made
unto salvation," to explain the essential need
for confession "of" one's sin, and repentance
"from" that same sin that separates man from
God. Note the requirement to "believe" that
Jesus is "Lord" and was raised "from the
dead." The transformation takes place in one's
"heart" through the act of total inner surrender to be followed by the proclamation of
Christ with the "mouth" to the world. It is not
accomplished by people through any act of his

or her own other than obedience; rather, it is the work of God in the heart of a willing and broken soul.

5. Finally, take the person to Romans 10:13, "Whoever calls on the name of the LORD shall be saved," to ask for an honest response from the person. Remember, while this is totally the work of the Holy Spirit, we should not be shy to ask for a response.

6. Leading to a response: If you sense that the Holy Spirit is at work and the person is connected and desires to surrender her or his heart and life to the Lordship of Jesus Christ, take a few moments to review what you have shared. As you do this, always explain the true meaning of what it is to be a Christ follower.

If the person is truly repentant and desires a relationship with Christ, you can utilize something similar to the following prayer as an example of what the person needs to communicate to Christ as she or he surrenders her or his life to Him:

Heavenly Father, I have sinned against you. I want forgiveness for all my sins. I believe that Jesus died on the cross for me and rose again. Father, I repent of my sins and surrender to you as Lord. From now on, my life is in your hands to do with as you wish. I want Jesus

Christ to come into my life and into my heart.
This I ask in Jesus' name, amen.

You can lead the person through the prayer phrase by phrase or you can simply ask the person to verbalize her or his desires to God in a similar manner. Once the person expresses heartfelt repentance to God, it is advisable for you to also lead in a prayer of celebration and thanksgiving for the salvation decision. Always remember that you cannot save anyone, it must be accomplished through the leadership of the Holy Spirit.

Other Suggested Approaches to Sharing Christ

Share Jesus Without Fear: A simple approach that uses a series of probing questions, combined with the Bible, that takes the fear out of sharing (www .sharejesuswithoutfear.com).

Got Life: An easy outline that utilizes the acrostic LIFE. It has a strong apologetics application within the overall presentation (www.gotlife.org).

The Way of the Master: Utilizes the Ten Commandments and a series of probing questions as a basis to establish "lostness" and present Christ (www .thewayofthemaster.com).

Evangecube: Great visual approach to sharing one's faith. Utilizes a small cube that is rotated to reveal one of four pictures representing the gospel message (www .simplysharejesus.com).

Counseling
Scott Hawkins

At some time or another everyone engages in counseling. It might be a friend who is struggling with a career decision who comes to you for advice or a friend who has questions about a relationship he or she is involved in. Other times the topic is more serious, such as a choice to continue to live or to end a marriage. The pastor may ask you to minister to a widow who recently lost her husband or a family with a wayward child. You are not a professional counselor in these situations nor are you in an official counseling relationship, but you are counseling.

This chapter will deal with the skills necessary to counsel, whether it is for the occasional times you counsel individuals or the times you are in a counseling relationship (more long term). This chapter will also guide you in developing an effective layperson counseling ministry within the local church. This can be a great aid to the pastoral staff who is overwhelmed with the counseling needs of the congregation.

Over and over again, hurt and broken individuals turn to the church as a place of sanctuary and healing. In order for this healing to be transformative it must be packaged in God's grace and truth. This chapter will seek to educate on the need for counseling in the church as well as create some helpful distinctions concerning the types of problems the church is equipped to deal with, as well as the types of problems that should be referred for professional counseling. The skillful application of God's word and the therapeutic truths within the helping relationship cannot only mend broken lives but develop mature Christians as well.

Establishing the Foundation

One of the most significant benefits of layperson counseling within the local church is the ability to understand and work with spiritual problems in the counselee's life. This may include relationship problems or deeper issues that interrupt the practice of fulfilling daily roles. So where does the counselor start in trying to understand and meet the needs of hurting people? A truth that I teach in various counseling classes is that we are a profoundly fallen people in a profoundly fallen world. What that means to us practically is that there has been a vandalism of shalom (personal peace) realized when Adam and Eve sinned in the garden of Eden. Unfortunately, as a result of the Fall we live in a world where the rain falls on the just and the unjust and bad things do happen to good people.

The Latin phrase *Imago Dei* means that we are created by God in His image and are of inherent worth as a result of being image bearers. As a layperson, this is important because in your counseling ministry you are in some cases assuming responsibility for guiding the direction of a person's life. You are not working with a car coming off an assembly line where a missing or misaligned piece results in a recall. Rather, you are working with individuals of incredible worth, created in the image of God, and deserving of our best efforts to give sound biblical solutions.

Understanding Basic Terminology

I have found it useful to think of problems as falling into one of several categories. Consider the following that describes problems on a continuum: chronically mentally ill, mental illness, the walking wounded, and the worried well. Lay counseling is particularly relevant for the "walking wounded" and "worried well" within our midst.

Keep in mind, however, that counseling has a language that is unique to its discipline and should be understood at a foundational level. This is essential if the lay counselor is going to be able to converse meaningfully with the church staff who will then pass on impressions to professionals in the counseling and medical fields. What will follow in this chapter will be an introduction to the basic terms as well as the essential skills utilized in lay counseling relationship.

The main issue is determining whether the church and its members can meet the needs of hurting people, or whether a professional referral is appropriate. When considering this decision, always remember two significant terms that should help in making this determination: "clinical significance" and "comorbidity."

"Clinical significance" is a term that describes problems that one encounters in life that interfere with a person's ability to live life at a fairly normal pace and routine. Whether intense grief, trauma, or a chemical imbalance, this person's life has become controlled or dominated by this malady. In most cases, clinically significant problems would incur a formal diagnosis and would greatly benefit from (if not require) professional counseling.

Now that we understand clinical significance, what does the term "comorbidity" mean? "Comorbidity" is a term used to describe a person who exemplifies the presence of more than one diagnosed problem at a time. For example, an individual who is drinking to excess has caused marital and physical problems, and likely legal challenges as well. Individuals who present a myriad of tough problems should be considered for professional referral. Appropriate treatment and management of these problems can then flow from an accurate assessment and treatment plan.

Understanding the Basics of Lay Counseling

For the sake of further examination, the remainder of this chapter will break down the counseling process.

The Therapeutic Relationship

In lay counseling there is one essential dynamic that research has shown to be the single most important ingredient for promoting positive change in the counseling process. That is, when a counselee develops a trusting relationship with the person he or she is working with, he or she is most likely to believe that positive change is possible.

Remember that you will be asking people to honestly examine their deepest secrets, darkest problems, and issues of sin. Thus, without a strong relational connection, the most basic goals of counseling cannot be achieved.

In addition, the most often-cited reason for dropping out of or discontinuing counseling stems from the counselee not developing a positive relationship with his or her counselor, even if it is a layperson. Oftentimes, it is this sense of teamwork that allows an individual to believe in a person's ability to change his or her life for the better. The point to be made here is found in the often-quoted saying "Nobody cares how much you know until they know how much you care."

With this in mind, there are several key areas of consideration that will aid in the creation of the therapeutic relationship or continue to strengthen it once established. These are some easily mastered skills that will make you, as a layperson, a better counselor. First, consider the manner in which you present yourself to the person you are helping. Adopt an open and interested posture that is inviting to the person and makes them comfortable with your presence. Thank the person for trusting you and project a warmth and desire to assist in the changes he or she is seeking to make. Maintain good eye contact as long as it does not violate any cultural taboos (some Asian cultures, for example, consider direct eye contact to be disrespectful). Consider not having anything between yourself and the person in order to prevent barriers, whether perceived or real, from forming between you and the counselee. Finally, if you and the counselee do not connect, you should be aware of other laypersons who are available for referral. If this is the case, match the person appropriately with someone of like gender, life experience, and personality to form the strongest alliance possible.

Find others in your church who have a heart for helping others and form a team. Discuss frankly the strengths and weaknesses that you possess as a lay ministry team and assign counselees based on compatibility and areas of strength. See if the church can budget monies that will pay for additional training such as cultural diversity, conflict resolution, and so forth, and search for and adopt helpful curriculum in problem areas including marriage, finances (Financial Peace University, www.daveramsey.com), or parenting (Chip Ingram, www.livingontheedge.org). Oftentimes, having the support of a solid curriculum is a comfort to both the counselor and the counselee. Using a basic curriculum also lends itself to productive homework assignments that will usually prompt deeper discussions.

Within the realm of the therapeutic relationship we will consider two more areas that directly influence the therapeutic alliance: ethics and confidentiality.

Your ethics govern not only the appropriate boundaries in the counseling relationship but also the very delivery of your approach as a counselor. The American Association of Christian Counselors has a downloadable code of ethics at its site (http://www.aacc.net /about-us/code-of-ethics) that you can refer to in familiarizing yourself with the ethical considerations involved in counseling. This is advisable, especially in lay counseling relationships. It is important for you to understand the ethics that govern your authority as a lay counselor in the church in order to avoid any unknowing or unintended breaches of ethical behavior.

Confidentiality is another fundamental concept when involving oneself as a lay counselor. Often confidentiality serves to create more freedom in the counseling process because the counselee can be honest and open without being concerned with having personal information repeated inappropriately.

There are, however, limits to confidentiality and they involve primarily incidents wherein the counselee discusses intent to harm herself or himself or someone else. This is also true when abuse is part of the equation. In these cases it is imperative that you are familiar with the reporting processes utilized in your state or local community. Oftentimes the social service department in your area will have an on-call worker whom you can contact and describe your situation to without divulging names in order to determine if it is a legally reportable situation.

In formal and ongoing situations, create a form for use in your lay counseling ministry that serves as a waiver of consent. In it you should outline all expectations for both the lay counselor and the counselee. You can also add your statement on confidentiality and the overall mission statement of your church. It is highly recommended that you then have your counselee sign it acknowledging that he or she has read and understood the document.

Furthermore, especially in a lay counseling situation, there needs to be systematic accountability when it comes to confidentiality and the need to report certain issues. When it comes to a counselee who has mentioned a desire to hurt himself or herself or others, it is advisable to call 911 to file an official report. In most states, you can also bring that individual to the local emergency room for observation and further determination about the most appropriate treatment.

Defining the Problem

"If you aim at nothing, you will hit it every time." In the counseling process, it is important to make sure that you define the problem that is to be addressed. Remember when we discussed comorbidity? It is important for you to note that counselees are often overwhelmed by life and its problems by the time they reach the point of seeking counseling. You can often make the process much more manageable by having the person start by telling his or her story, then clarifying the issues of greatest need.

It is important to note that if you encourage the counselee to tell his or her story then you must give the person the opportunity to tell that story in its entirety. Oftentimes, if you try to ask questions, edit, or interact with counselees as they tell their stories you can have the unintended consequence of shutting someone down. Take notes if you are concerned you will not remember details, but let the person tell the story from start to finish. This is often a cathartic (cleansing) experience in and of itself, and will usually result in a greater awareness on the part of the counselee.

There are several important reasons for having the client identify the problem. First, there is the issue of ownership. When the counselee identifies the problem he or she is more likely to own the problem and be open to suggested remedies. Second, the counselee is more likely to recognize personal benefit from the process and therefore more likely to listen and respond in a positive manner.

Once you get the person to identify the problem, work toward having the counselee join you in the "here and now." What this means in practice is to have the person intently shut out the world in order to focus on the problem and its resolution. Encourage the person to leave work and home problems for that period of time and, if possible, to turn off cell phones or pagers, so he or she can be entirely focused on attacking the problem. I once watched a couple in marital therapy constantly texting as we were trying to work through some important issues. When I gently confronted them about putting the phones away I realized that the husband had been text-ing the wife to tell her how to answer the questions that I had been posing to the couple.

Assess the Commitment to Change

Assessing the person's commitment to change is important in that it helps the lay counselor to choose his or her approach to the person. A counselee who is com-mitted to change can be approached more supportively, can be nurtured through the growth process, and often needs an educational approach that is rooted in grace. The resistant counselee, on the other hand, has to be confronted often with the truth of the impending conse-quences of their continued poor decision making.

There is a warning. This truth-based approach often feels very confrontational to the counselee and the coun-selor must make a significant effort to instill both the hope of and need for change within the counselee's life. The lay counselor needs to become attuned to the ways in which a person demonstrates a resistance to help. Some of these forms of resistance include denial, an unwillingness to do homework, skipped meetings, and an argumentative or combative attitude. Resistant coun-selees are often frustrating. In some cases, all you can do is sow the seed of truth and trust that there will be a harvest at some point in the counselee's life. Especially in the area of addictions, a counselee often has to hit rock bottom before the truths of God's Word and the consequences of their actions combine to create a heart condition wherein they are willing to make the necessary changes.

Assessing a person's willingness to change provides the lay counselor with some feedback on how to approach and pace the counseling process. It is always advisable to find the areas in the person's life that act as motivators for change (spouse, children, job, and standing in the community or church) and focus your interventions on those areas or the consequences that will be felt in those areas if the counselee does not make the needed changes. If the person continues to be resistant, a lay counselor should always consult the church staff/pastor to determine if he or she should discontinue working with the person. In some cases, it will be best to let the church staff determine the best course of action.

Goal Setting

Goal setting is an important part of the lay counseling process. One of the more important aspects of goal setting is the creation of hope. When the person is able to see and feel tangible progress toward resolving personal problems, she or he develops a sense of optimism that helps energize the need to seek healing.

Goal setting is about possibilities—possibilities for a better tomorrow and a better future. Goal setting is important because it attempts to move the person from a problem-centered focus to a problem-solving focus. Goal setting involves "brainstorming" the possibilities for a different, more desirable outcome than the person is currently experiencing. Goal setting is helpful because it is future focused and involves entertaining the possibility of success as opposed to experiencing continued failure.

As with defining the problem, try to get the person to take ownership for setting and owning personal goals. This is one way of attacking the resistance to change that we just talked about. Also, it teaches the person an active, problem-solving skill that he or she can retain and use throughout life. As the lay counselor, try to ensure that the person's goals are realistic, measurable, and attainable. Try to avoid situations where the person sets goals that are overly ambitious.

Goal setting should be used to strengthen the counseling relationship, address the identified problem, and start allowing the counselee to experience small successes. A good goal needs to be specific—think in terms of who, what, where, when, and how in order to create a specific, measurable goal. A goal needs to motivate and challenge the person you are assisting while still being attainable. As the lay counselor, always remember the goals and revisit them often. Furthermore, create opportunities to challenge the person's progress regularly, and facilitate changes in goals when they become necessary to motivate growth.

Basic Counseling Skills

What are some of the more concrete skills that you might utilize as a lay counselor? Even though it is not expected for a lay counselor to become a professional psychologist, it will not hurt to understand some of the basic underlying happenings that occur in many counseling situations. While by no means a comprehensive list, consider learning and developing the skills outlined below.

Transference occurs in the counseling relationship when the individual develops feelings for the counselor or the person working with him or her. These feelings can be positive or negative and range from love to hate. It is generally accepted that transference occurs because the counselor reminds the counselee of someone in the person's life—past or present—because of looks, personality, or mannerisms. Transference can help or harm the process and the lay counselor needs to recognize the possibility and be honest when it is taking place. If you are not sure if your counselee is experiencing transference, seek advice from the pastor.

Countertransference occurs when the counselor shares the counselee's feelings from transference or develops feelings for the counselee based on the same rationale outlined in the definition of transference. Often transference and countertransference are unavoidable and even a natural part of the process. As the lay counselor, clarify with the counselee the person's honest feelings and make sure that you have strong, appropriate (accountable) boundaries to guide your actions. You may also consider finding someone else to work with the person if her or his feelings are prohibitively negative or if you feel the ability to continue in a productive manner has been compromised. This is especially dangerous if you are not honest about feelings of attraction, among others. If there is any hesitation, contact your pastor and find someone else to follow up with the person.

Paraphrasing is a way to connect with the person by summarizing (repeating) what he or she has just said in order to demonstrate comprehension and good listening skills. If your paraphrase is inaccurate, the person has the opportunity to clarify what was said as you progress in the conversation. You will find that listening with the intent to comprehend and verbally paraphrase will make you a much better counselor.

Like paraphrasing, attending is centered on the person and shows empathy, genuineness, and positive regard for your counselee. Attending behaviors include your nonverbal behaviors such as displaying an open posture, smiling, and nodding, as well as verbal behaviors such as affirming, agreeing, and nurturing. Attending behaviors reassure the person that she or he is doing the gut-wrenching work of looking at her or his problems honestly. This process supports and encourages the person's efforts.

Silence can be an incredibly powerful skill to possess and use appropriately as a lay counselor. On the whole, we are a society that is uncomfortable with silence. Conversationally, we often feel awkward if someone is shy when it comes to verbal communication. This is especially true when we are in a counseling mode. Actually, silence is a powerful skill and is sometimes necessary and helpful for keeping us from offering set answers or inadequate replies to tragic situations and circumstances. Relax, pray, and listen.

In fact, I remember sitting next to a dear friend as he came to grips with the loss of his stillborn daughter in the eighth month of pregnancy. I had no helpful words to convey my anguish for his situation, so I sat next to him in silence for an hour and a half. He finally turned to me and hugged me and said "thank you." I asked him why he was thanking me and he said it was for just being there, not trying to fix everything, and not offering him advice that would probably serve to make him angrier and more confused.

Disclosure refers to the sharing of your personal life with the counselee. Sometimes an appropriate disclosure can strengthen the relationship and provide the nudge that allows the person to break through an impasse. Disclosure can also cement your authority or credibility with the person. While not essential, when appropriate, stating, "I've been there and I've done that. I know what you're feeling right now," can oftentimes lead to greater vulnerability and growth on the part of the counselee. The key is honest empathy and authentic compassion.

Confronting is a necessary skill that is a part of ministering grace and truth to the person. When you confront, always focus on the problem and not the individual. In the process of confronting you need to manage your emotions in a productive and professional manner. Remember that one of your responsibilities is to be an appropriate model of Christian love and compassion. I like to use a "positive sandwich" approach whenever possible to address conflict. The idea is to place the confrontation, or negative comment, in the middle of two positive comments. It would look something like this: "I have seen you working so hard in this area and have seen great results. The problem is that in this other area, you seem to be struggling more than ever. I know that if you will bring the same focus to this area you will be successful here as well."

Assessment is a learned skill and it actually needs to be done throughout the entire length of the counseling process. For instance, you should assess the person's ownership of his or her problem—the person's commitment, resistance, well-being, and spiritual sensitivity throughout the entire counseling process. Assessment is the key factor leading to the final step: termination. One other note on assessment: be aware that there exists a multitude of (online) inventories and questionnaires to assist you in the assessment process.

Active listening requires discipline and concentration. As a lay counselor, you need to work in the here and now, following the same practice you are asking from the counselees. Make sure that you are not distracted and that you give the person your full attention during sessions. Do not try to do other things like answer phones or text. Active listening involves paying attention to your verbal and nonverbal conversation and behaviors. One suggestion is to practice summarizing in your head what you have discussed with the person after the session is over to see how much you can recall. Bottom line, if you do not practice active listening, you will miss windows of opportunity to speak grace and truth into your counselee's life.

Ask open-ended questions. A closed question is one that does not require meaningful dialogue to be answered, and is usually answered with a simple yes or no. An open-ended question is one that requires dialogue from the other person. Open-ended questions are useful for drawing out and gaining insight into what people truly are thinking and feeling. Let me suggest that you practice crafting open-ended questions and direct them to friends before using them on a person you are counseling. If the person answers yes or no, keep trying.

An example of an open-ended question you might pose is "When I am stressed I tend to ...."

Empathy is the skill that involves seeing others with the eyes and heart of Christ. When Jesus met the woman at the well in John 4, He did not judge or condemn her. Rather, even more powerful, by understanding (empathizing with) her situation, he created a set of life-changing expectations. As a result, a whole city (Samaria) was given the opportunity for spiritual healing.

In addition, consider how Jesus responded in John 8:3–11 (KJV):

> ³And the scribes and Pharisees brought unto him a woman taken in adultery; and when they had set her in the midst, ⁴They say unto him, Master, this woman was taken in adultery, in the very act. ⁵Now Moses in the law commanded us, that such should be stoned: but what sayest thou? ⁶This they said, tempting him, that they might have to accuse him.

But Jesus stooped down, and with his finger wrote on the ground, as though he heard them not. [7] So when they continued asking him, he lifted up himself, and said unto them, He that is without sin among you, let him first cast a stone at her. [8] And again he stooped down, and wrote on the ground. [9] And they which heard it, being convicted by their own conscience, went out one by one, beginning at the eldest, even unto the last: and Jesus was left alone, and the woman standing in the midst. [10] When Jesus had lifted up himself, and saw none but the woman, he said unto her, Woman, where are those thine accusers? hath no man condemned thee? [11] She said, No man, Lord. And Jesus said unto her, Neither do I condemn thee: go, and sin no more.

Jesus was empathetically interested in transforming the woman's life. While He did not condone her sin, He did not condemn her either. In the end, the woman refers to Jesus as "Lord" and is given a new lease on life to "go, and sin no more."

Empathy is attempting to walk in the other person's shoes, really seeking to understand what that person is experiencing. Sympathy, on the other hand, is more in line with feeling sorry for the other person because of what he or she is experiencing. Empathy is an essential counseling skill to master because it allows you to meet the person where he or she is in life without passing judgment. True compassion always creates expectations for change and growth.

Unconditional positive regard means genuinely caring about the person and being able to convey that care in a way that is tangible to the counselee. This literally is seeing the person as created in the image of God and thus possessing incredible worth. Unconditional positive regard conveys to the counselee that the time you are spending with her or him is time well spent, and moreover that she or he is worthy of that time.

Romans 15:1–6 describes this selfless approach to the counselee:

> [1] We then who are strong ought to bear with the scruples of the weak, and not to please ourselves. [2] Let each of us please his neighbor for his good, leading to edification. [3] For even Christ did not please Himself; but as it is written, "The reproaches of those who reproached You fell on Me." [4] For whatever things were written before were written for our learning, that we through the patience and comfort of the Scriptures might have hope. [5] Now may the God of patience and comfort grant you to be like-minded toward one another, according to Christ Jesus, [6] that you may with one mind and one mouth glorify the God and Father of our Lord Jesus Christ.

Sometimes what your counselee needs is the simple gift of your presence. Remember the use of silence?

Sometimes, in the midst of a crisis, your presence can have a calming effect. Always remember that we are to be modeling Christ. As a lay counselor, your presence should serve as a model for your counselee to observe and follow.

Try to instill hope. Do you recall the poem about the footprints in the sand? Two sets of footprints turn into one and then after a distance, back to two. Written in 1936 by fourteen-year-old Mary Stevenson, this poem represents times in our life when God had to carry us because we did not have the strength to continue on our own. I love this poem because it accurately describes our role in the lives of hurting people when we choose to help them as lay counselors.

Case in point: in Jeremiah 29:11–13, God talks about this same desire for us:

> [11] For I know the thoughts that I think toward you, says the LORD, thoughts of peace and not of evil, to give you a future and a hope. [12] Then you will call upon Me and go and pray to Me, and I will listen to you. [13] And you will seek Me and find Me, when you search for Me with all your heart.

A necessary part of our job as lay counselors is to instill and maintain hope in the hearts and minds of the people we serve. We need to believe in our counselee's ability to change if they will put God first in their lives. This belief instills them with the energy and necessary hope to tough it out as God works in their lives.

Terminating the Counseling Relationship

Terminating the counseling relationship can be as emotional for you as it is for the person you have served. You have invested selflessly in the form of time, energy, and emotion. Now it is time to let go and watch the individual put into practice everything you have discussed.

Beware. There can be a real sense of loss at this juncture. As the lay counselor, I recommend that you talk about termination from the first time you meet. Ask questions like "How will you know when we have finished our work together?" or "What will that look and feel like in your life?"

Essential Ingredients to Christian Counseling

As a lay counselor there are three more essential ingredients to a good Christian counseling ministry through the local church. They are the Bible, prayer, and the Holy Spirit. Each ingredient is foundational for all Christian counseling.

The Bible is the inerrant, inspired Word of God. In a day in which society would like to avoid absolutes, the Bible remains our authoritative final truth on any given subject. Hebrews 4:12 says: "For the word of God is living and powerful, and sharper than any two-edged sword, piercing even to the division of soul and spirit, and of joints and marrow, and is a discerner of the thoughts and intents of the heart." Additionally, consider 2 Timothy 3:16–17: "All Scripture is given by inspiration of God, and is profitable for doctrine, for reproof, for correction, for instruction in righteousness, that the man of God may be complete, thoroughly equipped for every good work."

Our authority in Christian counseling must remain rooted in the Word of God. The lay counselor needs to be well grounded in the Scriptures as noted in 1 Peter 3:15: "But sanctify the Lord God in your hearts, and always be ready to give a defense to everyone who asks you a reason for the hope that is in you, with meekness and fear." The word of God is an essential tool for quickening and convicting the heart and mind of the counselee in the therapeutic process.

Prayer is also an essential component of the process. Even when working with unsaved couples, you can bathe your time and your counsel in prayer. Ephesians 6:18 says one should be "praying always with all prayer and supplication in the Spirit, being watchful to this end with all perseverance and supplication for all the saints." Prayer is incredibly powerful in the counseling process and is one skill that needs to be taught, modeled, and encouraged as part of the counselee's healing and growth. It is wise for a lay counselor to become familiar with the Psalms and learn the many facets, types, and applications of prayer in educating the counselee.

The Holy Spirit must be welcomed into the counseling session as the chief agent for positive growth and change. John 16:7–8 says:

> [7] Nevertheless I tell you the truth. It is to your advantage that I go away; for if I do not go away, the Helper will not come to you; but if

> I depart, I will send Him to you. [8] And when
> He has come, He will convict the world of sin,
> and of righteousness, and of judgment.

As a lay counselor, do everything possible to invite the Holy Spirit into the counseling session. When this verse talks about the Holy Spirit and says that he will convict the world of sin, it unleashes the potential for an incredibly powerful ally to change people's lives. As you facilitate truth and grace, the Holy Spirit convicts and makes real the counsel that you are offering.

These are ten helpful hints for the lay counselor:

1. Always seek to work under the authority and accountability of the local church.

2. In this same vein, seek the advice of the senior pastor and staff. Keep them informed.

3. Do not allow opportunities for counseling to become gripe sessions that will ultimately destroy the local church. Practice Matthew 18.

4. Realize that you are not a professional counselor. Know your limits.

5. Familiarize yourself with the "transference" and "countertransference" concepts in order to maintain healthy emotional relationships.

6. It is generally suggested that lay counselors should only advise people of the same sex in order to protect long-term integrity and to

avoid moral temptations. If you are meeting with someone of the opposite sex, be sure you do not meet in an isolated area. Do not meet with the person for meals or in places that could send the wrong message to the individual or others who see you. If you are married and are working with someone of the opposite sex, get permission to tell your spouse and invite your spouse to join you.

7. Understand pertinent legal issues such as reporting abuse or suicidal behavior. Your pastor can help you with this.

8. Listen with your ears and eyes.

9. Practice compassion over judgment.

10. Most of all, it is good for you to be willing to serve in this mode, but you must know your limitations and be quick to refer the individual elsewhere whenever you feel overwhelmed or uncomfortable. Your pastor is a great resource.

As a lay counselor, always remember that you are God's vessel for truth and grace to hurting people. Therefore, you must be spiritually healthy and willing to be accountable to church leadership. Lay counseling can be frustrating and emotionally draining, especially if it drags out for a long time period. You have to be careful to avoid burnout and moral failure. With that said, seeing individuals and families being transformed through the counseling process is an incredibly fulfilling and rewarding opportunity to assist the pastor and staff by ministering through the local church.

Part Three
Caring for Hurting People

Conflict
Kent Spann

Blessed are the peacemakers, for they shall be called sons of God.

—Matthew 5:9

Overview

Simply the mention of the word *conflict* creates an uneasy feeling. We do not like conflict, so we do all we can to avoid it. But the reality is that conflict is inevitable. It is inevitable at work, in marriage, and yes, even in the church. It is inevitable between unbelievers and just as inevitable between believers.

The Bible is full of examples of conflict between people: Cain and Abel (Gen. 4), Abram and Lot (Gen. 13), Joseph and his brothers (Gen. 37), David and Saul (1 Sam. 18), the disciples (Luke 22:24), Paul and Barnabas (Acts 15:36–41), and Euodia and Syntyche (Phil. 4:2–3). There are also stories of conflict between parties or groups as well as between people and leadership: Moses and Israel (Ex. 15:22–24), and Joshua and Caleb and the other spies (Num. 13:26–14:38). Even the early church had conflict (Acts 15).

Conflict Defined

What is conflict? Ken Sande, in his book *The Peacemaker*, defines conflict as "a difference in opinion or purpose that frustrates someone's goals or desires."[22] Gary Collins says, "Conflict involves a struggle that occurs when two or more people have goals that appear to be incompatible, or when they want something that is scarce."[23] Sometimes it is a conflict between organizations or groups but even then it is a conflict between persons because organizations or groups are made up of people.

Sources of Conflict

It is important to know the three basic sources of conflict. They are often inseparable but it is still helpful to differentiate the sources: Satan, people, and groups.

As believers, we cannot underestimate the influence of Satan in creating conflict. In the very beginning, he was involved in creating conflict among Adam, Eve, and God (Gen. 3). While we cannot blame him as the sole source of conflict, we must acknowledge his part in most conflict.

People are a source of conflict because conflict is between two or more people. There can be many factors at play in a conflict. Below are just a few.

1. People can be in conflict because they are operating in the flesh (pride, fear, bitterness, anger, self-centeredness, etc.). See Galatians 5:19–26 and James 4:1–3.

2. People can be in conflict because of misunderstandings. Many times conflict occurs because of differences in God-given personalities and even spiritual gifts. Each sees life or a situation

from his or her perspective, while failing to see it from the other person's. Sometimes it occurs because of poor communication, which leads to misunderstandings.

3. People can be in conflict because of differing values and beliefs.

4. People operate in social networks. These social networks can be friendships, organizations, churches, Sunday school classes, or leadership teams. Groups play a powerful role in people's lives and thus exert great influence. Behind many conflicts will be group thinking or belief.

The Role of Peacemaker

Conflict will be one of the most prominent issues you will deal with as a person engaged in caring for others. Just a few of the conflicts you may be called upon to mediate are marital conflicts, personal conflicts, leadership conflicts, church conflicts, and sometimes even business conflicts. What is your role? The Bible makes it very clear: you are called to be a peacemaker (Prov. 12:20; Matt. 5:9; Rom. 14:19; Phil. 4:2–3).

There are many examples of peacemakers in the Bible (1 Sam. 25:18–35; Esther; Acts 9:26–28) but the most powerful is the Lord Jesus Christ. His mission on earth was to make peace between man and man (Eph. 2:14–15), but most important, between man and God (Eph. 2:16–22). He accomplished both through the instrument of the cross. As followers of Christ, we are to model his life, which means being peacemakers.

What Is Your Role as a Peacemaker?

Model being a peacemaker (Rom. 12:18; Heb. 12:14). Your credibility as a peacemaker is determined by how you deal with the conflicts in your own life. You need to practice the biblical principles of conflict resolution. A peacemaker has to get the plank out of his or her own eye before he or she can help others (Matt. 7:3–5). Start with resolving conflicts in your personal life.

Bring together the individuals or groups in conflict. That was Paul's exhortation to the "loyal yokefellow" in Philippians 4:3 (NIV). Conflict separates; the peacemaker seeks to reunite.

Help the persons in conflict find a solution that is biblical and practical. Many times, as a third party you are able to see a solution that has been clouded by the conflict between the two individuals. That is what the apostles did when a conflict arose in the early church (Acts 6:1–7). Confront sin when there is a lack of repentance (Prov. 25:12; 27:5–6; Gal. 2:11–14). Love the individuals even if they do not reconcile (John 13:34–35). Pray for peace (Phil. 4:6–7).

Just a few words of caution to the peacemaker:

1. Guard against absorbing bitterness (Heb. 12:15). Bitterness infects others, even the peacemaker. You can easily find yourself taking up an offense.

2. Hear both sides before forming your opinions or giving advice (Prov. 18:17).

3. Be careful not to get drawn into the conflict or, even worse, get caught in the middle of the conflict.

4. Know your limits.

Your goal as a peacemaker is to help others make peace with one another, which glorifies God (1 Cor. 10:31). When unity is preserved by reconciliation and restoration then God is ultimately glorified (John 17:1–26). Of course, you will not be able to resolve all conflicts. Paul acknowledged that in Romans 12:18: "If it is possible, as much as depends on you, live peaceably with all men." Even the apostle Paul could not resolve some conflicts (Acts 15:39). Do not be discouraged or give up as a peacemaker when the process is unsuccessful. Remember God does not hold you accountable for the results, just your faithfulness and obedience to Him.

Ministry Strategy

So how do we deal with conflict? The goal is to prevent conflict from causing harm to the parties involved in the conflict as well as collateral damage to others who are not involved.

This section will provide some very simple strategies for dealing with conflict. Obviously, every aspect of conflict cannot be covered in so short a chapter. If you take the role of peacemaker seriously, you need to do further study of the Scriptures and other resources.

Pray

This is not a pious platitude. You need to pray because it is a war out there (Eph. 6:10–20). You need to pray because reconciliation is a divine work (Eph. 2:14). You need to pray because you need divine wisdom (Col. 1:9; James 1:5). Pray before meeting with the person(s), pray with the person(s), and pray after the meeting.

Listen Well

This is important when talking with one of the people in the conflict or when you have both parties in the room. The tendency is to start giving answers. Many times talking it out will help the individual or the parties resolve the difference. Good listening means asking good questions, clearly understanding the issues, not passing judgment, and respecting the individual talking.

Determine the Cause of the Conflict

There are basically two causes of conflict: a sinful action (Matt. 18:15–20; James 4:1–3) or a difference (Acts 15:36–39). Sometimes there will be a clear sinful action that leads to the conflict. For example, if a person lied about an individual, which led to the conflict, then the cause of the conflict is sin. If someone cheated another, then the cause of the conflict is sin.

Contrary to popular belief, not all conflict is caused by sin. All conflict can become sin, however, if not dealt with properly. Sometimes conflict is caused by differences of ideas, opinions, philosophies, preferences, outlooks, or goals, which are not necessarily sinful. Many of these conflicts are elevated to the level of a spiritual conflict when in truth they are just differences between two people or groups. A classic example is music in the church. A conflict about music in the church is really about preferences, not right or wrong.

It is important to determine the cause because the courses of action are different.

Promote Reconciliation

Reconciliation was the message and prayer of Jesus (Matt. 5:23–24; 18:15–20; John 17:20–23). It was also the message of Paul (Phil 4:2–3; Philemon).

Here are a few things that promote reconciliation: getting the plank out of one's eye (Matt. 7:3–5), humility (Phil. 2:3–4), forbearing in love or agreeing to disagree in love (Eph. 4:2), practicing Christian love (1 Cor. 13), and listening to the other person instead of getting angry (James 1:19–20).

Forgiveness has two aspects. The first is asking forgiveness when a person is wrong (Prov. 28:13; Luke 15:18). As a peacemaker, you will need to help the person think through how to correctly ask for forgiveness (Prov. 24:6) as well as recognize the correct timing to ask forgiveness (Prov. 25:11). The second aspect of forgiveness is granting forgiveness (Matt. 6:12, 14–15; Col. 3:13). You will need to help the individual(s) practice good biblical forgiveness because, from what I have seen, most believers do not know how to forgive.

Overlook an offense (Prov. 10:12; 17:9; 19:11). Sometimes the best thing a person can do is to overlook an offense rather than turn it into a conflict. Not every offense warrants a conflict.

Guard the tongue (James 3:1–12). The sins of the tongue such as gossip, slander, backbiting, and so forth create and elevate conflict. They must be avoided. Do not seek revenge; rather, do good (Rom. 12:19–21).

Go to the Church Leadership

There may be times that, because of the seriousness of the conflict, you will need to go to the church leadership with the issue, if one or both of the parties refuses to reconcile (Matt. 18:16–17). Such times would be, for example, if the reputation of the church and Christ is being affected by the conflict or if the conflict seriously threatens the unity of the church.

Refer to a Professional

Sometimes the conflict is too complicated or it involves a legal matter. In those cases you need to refer the persons to a competent Christian counselor or lawyer who can help them resolve their differences.

Glorify God

At the end of the day, you as the peacemaker and those in conflict must remember that the most important thing is to glorify God (Matt. 5:16; 1 Cor. 10:31). Everyone should be asking how they can please and honor God in the situation.

Divorce
Kent Spann

4 And He answered and said to them, "Have you not read that He who made them at the beginning 'made them male and female,' 5 and said, 'For this reason a man shall leave his father and mother and be joined to his wife, and the two shall become one flesh'? 6 So then, they are no longer two but one flesh. Therefore what God has joined together, let not man separate."

—Matthew 19:4–6

Overview

Divorce is a difficult and even touchy subject not only in current society but also in the church. It is difficult because it is so personal and painful. It affects every aspect of a person's life, emotionally, relationally, mentally, financially, vocationally sometimes, parentally, and even spiritually.

While it is a difficult subject, it is a very real issue in our day. What is troubling is that according to the Barna Research Group, the divorce rates among evangelical and non-evangelical Christians is identical to the non-Christian population.[24]

Our current society has definitely made divorce more acceptable as well as easy to obtain. What society has not been able to do is minimize the effect of divorce.

Divorce has a ripple effect, affecting society, the family structure, the financial stability of nation, children (emotionally, educationally, etc.), the church, and spirituality.

The Bible and Divorce

The Scriptures are very clear on what God says about divorce. Divorce goes against God's plan and purpose for marriage (Matt. 19:4–6). No passage is clearer than Malachi 2:16 where God states he hates divorce. God is not saying that He hates the one who is divorced, rather, He is saying He hates the act of divorce because it goes against the marriage covenant (Mal. 2:14).

Divorce is not God's plan but it is a reality of the fallen world in which we live. It is going to happen, thus Moses permitted it, and Jesus affirmed it (Matt. 19:8–9). The Scriptures do not give one carte blanche to divorce. It is at this point that differing interpretations come into play. Within the church and among Christians, there are different interpretations of divorce. Gary Collins, in his book *Christian Counseling*, states the four categories that views fall into:

> First are those who conclude that marriage is for life, that divorce is never permitted on biblical grounds, and that remarriage of a divorced person always is adultery. Second, some conclude that there are legitimate biblical grounds for divorce and remarriage, including desertion and adultery, wherein one person has been left by a spouse who has

had sexual intercourse outside of the marriage and has no desire to reconcile. Third is the view that some circumstances arise in marriage that defy solution. Divorce then becomes necessary for the sake of the mental, emotional, or physical health of one of the spouses or their children. This view is based less on specific biblical teaching and more on general biblical principles of compassion and sensitivity. Fourth is a view held mostly by Roman Catholic writers, that a church court can annul a marriage and thus pave the way for remarriage.[25]

You are encouraged to talk with your church leaders to determine the church's view on divorce and remarriage. You will need to decide on your position. If your position is different from your church's and you are representing your church, you need to honor the position of the church or at least discuss where you are with your church leadership.

The purpose of this chapter is not to espouse one of the views over another; rather, it is to consider how to minister to hurting people in the reality of the world in which we live.

Ministry Strategy

At some time or another, you will find yourself dealing with the issue of divorce as you care for people. You will minister to people in one or all of the categories below.

Before Divorce

Bill calls and says he wants to meet you for lunch. While you sit, expecting an enjoyable lunch, Bill drops the bombshell that Susie and he are getting a divorce. It has not happened yet but they are considering it or moving in that direction. In another scenario, you receive news that Bob and Michelle are considering divorce. You call to see if you can meet with them.

At this stage your role is to intervene to save the marriage. The following is a list of things you can do. They are not necessarily in any order, because every situation will be unique, depending on how you find out about the potential divorce, who set up the meeting, whether you are talking with one or both spouses, the circumstances behind the divorce (adultery, abuse, conflict, depression, etc.), and where you are in the process of dealing with the person or couple. Trust the Holy Spirit to guide you. The most important thing you can do is pray. This is at its heart a spiritual battle (Eph. 6:10–19). Satan's goal is to destroy the home.

In the beginning, let the individual or the couple talk it out with you. It is important to hear both sides and to avoid passing judgment (Prov. 18:17). Encourage them to slow down (Prov. 19:2; 21:5). The worst thing the couple or spouse can do is move with haste or impulsively. Of course, it is not something the person just thought of. At this stage the option of divorce has been on the table for quite a while. You are counseling them to slow down on acting on it.

Get them to agree to talk with the pastor or a counselor (Prov. 11:14; 24:6). Offer to go with them if they would like. For some, the thought of talking with a pastor or counselor is intimidating. Follow up to make sure they met with the pastor or counselor.

If they are Christians, get them to consider what the Scriptures teach about divorce, forgiveness, reconciliation, hope, and God's power to change lives and marriages (see Scriptures at the end). Avoid using Scripture to condemn them. Let the Holy Spirit (John 16:8–11) and Scripture (Heb. 4:12) work in the couples' hearts.

Promote reconciliation as God's will for the believer. While divorce is permitted, it is not God's perfect will. Point out that divorce is not the easy way out. If there are children, the children will suffer. Everyone's lives will change more than they will ever realize and in ways they do not expect. It will not mean the end of problems, stress, and difficulties. The truth is, many times the problems, stresses, and difficulties will increase. If, for instance, financial difficulties are at the heart of the conflict, divorce will not alleviate them; the truth is it will magnify them. The person or couple simply trades one set of hardships and difficulties for another set that may be worse. The individuals will not necessarily be any happier. According to a study of unhappy marriages,[26] on average unhappily married adults who divorced were no happier than unhappily married adults who stayed married, when rated on any of twelve separate measures of psychological well-being.

If there is abuse or threat to life, encourage the spouse to seek safety and get appropriate help. In some cases she or he may need to get legal help from police or the courts.

If there is adultery, see the chapter in this book on conflict. Seek permission to alert your pastor or church leadership about the situation. There are different views in the case of separation, so know your church's stance. Separation can be helpful but usually only if the couple is involved in mediation or counseling. Without someone holding them together, a couple may find the separation makes it easier for them to divorce, because there is a temporary relief of problems and stress. Pray, pray, pray.

When it is all said and done, remember you are not a professional counselor. You are simply there to offer care, compassion, and assistance. By the time a couple gets to this point, many times it is hard to get them to change course because the problems have been building for a long time. The circumstances that lead people to seek divorce do not happen overnight.

After Divorce

Divorce is going to happen. It is critically important to minister to those who have been through divorce. Another thing to remember is that divorce is not the unpardonable sin. It can be forgiven. Forgiveness, however, is not an excuse for divorce.

After a divorce, your role is helping the person put his or her life back together again. It may involve helping the children who are struggling through their parents' divorce. Let the person know that divorce is the end of a marriage but not the end of his or her life. God can put any life back together, when the individual surrenders to Him.

Encourage the person to go to counseling or get in a support group such as a divorce recovery group in a local church. There are issues the person needs to work through lest she or he repeat the same mistakes or carry current pain into a future relationship. If the person cannot afford counseling or there are no official support groups, ask the church leadership to set up a team of people to act as a support group.

Help the individual to understand he or she is going through a grieving process (see the chapter on grief). Discover what the person's practical needs are. For instance, a woman may not know about taking care of her car because her husband did that. The divorced may need help with children. Many times there are financial needs.

Caution the recently divorced against getting into a relationship too quickly. The loneliness and emptiness can be overwhelming at times. Many times the person will move right into another relationship. This is not good because the person has not worked through issues of grief and discovered what went wrong in the last relationship. If a recently divorced person goes right into another relationship, he or she will bring all those mistakes and feelings into the next one. That is why the statistics show that as many as 75 percent of second marriages end in divorce. Andrew Cherlin, a Johns Hopkins sociologist and author of the book *The Marriage-Go-Round* says of Americans, "We divorce, repartner, and remarry faster than people in any other country."[27]

Love the person. A person needs to know she or he is still loved. Be with the person as he or she transitions into a new life (Prov. 18:24; 27:10). There will be the loss of friends because many of the person's friends are couples. Encourage and help the person find a single's group or divorce class in the church he or she can attend if he or she is not comfortable going to his or her former married class.

Be honest with the individual (Prov. 27:14; Eph. 4:15). She or he is hurting, but silence will not help if she or he is about to make a decision or do something that could hurt or be detrimental to the person or the person's children.

Be alert to danger signals like major depression or suicidal thoughts. Report any such things to the appropriate person or authority.

If the person you are dealing with is the cause of divorce due to pornography, adultery, abuse, or so on, consult with your church leadership concerning how you should proceed. Also see chapters on sexual violence and sexual addiction. Pray, pray, pray. Remember you are not a professional counselor.

Scripture

Divorce: Deuteronomy 24:1–4; Malachi 2:13–16; Matthew 5:31–32; 19:1–12; Mark 10:1–12; Luke 16:18; 1 Corinthians 7:10–16

Anxiety and Fear: Psalm 56:10–11; Matthew 6:25–34; 2 Timothy 1:7; Hebrews 13:5–6; 1 John 4:18

Forgiving others and reconciliation: Matthew 5:21–26; Mark 11:25; Ephesians 4:32; Colossians 3:13

Receiving God's forgiveness: Psalms 51; 103:1–3; 130:4; Ephesians 1:7; 1 John 1:9

Other Scripture topics: God's love, the will of God, hope, marriage, speech and faith

Eating Disorders
Cindy Spann

5 Trust in the LORD with all your heart
    and lean not on your own understanding;
6 in all your ways acknowledge him,
    and he will make your paths straight.
7 Do not be wise in your own eyes;
    fear the LORD and shun evil.
8 This will bring health to your body
    and nourishment to your bones.

—Proverbs 3:5–8 (NIV)

"I will show them, I am not going to be fat!" was the innocent statement I said to myself when I was a sophomore in high school. At 5'6" and 138 pounds I thought I was fat. It was at this point that I started on a journey and a quest to lose weight. I loved the control that I had, and the attention that I got as I lost weight. Being a perfectionist, which is a common trait among people with eating disorders, I still thought I had to be thin and successful in everything even though I felt secure and accepted by family and friends. As you can see, I had a warped self-image and had no clue who I was in Christ. I reached 110 pounds and had physical problems for two years. I eventually transitioned from having anorexia to having bouts of bulimia, which further jeopardized my health.

Overview

What is an eating disorder? An eating disorder is an illness, and it requires professional counseling and medical attention. It is not an illness like the flu or diabetes that is purely physiological. It is an illness because it is an unhealthy condition with many contributing factors and issues including the physiological, mental, and spiritual. Eating disorders include a myriad of types and styles with no set dynamics among them, but they all include a preoccupation with food and a distorted self-image. This usually results from feeling out of control and wanting to gain a sense of well-being. It can be rather overwhelming, so I am going to focus on those disorders that are truly life threatening. The two types of eating disorders that I want to target are anorexia nervosa and bulimia nervosa. From my own experience, a person can transition from anorexia to bulimia at any point in the illness. People from each of these groups suffer differently and have different characteristics and medical complications. All ages and sexes are affected, but young women are usually the ones to succumb to this illness. They are driven daily to be "thin," and it does not help to simply tell them to "just eat" or to "get control." When there is the slightest weight gain, the person becomes even more obsessed with food intake and exercise regimen. Due to the guilt from the weight gain, the vicious cycle of starvation or of bingeing and purging continues. As you can see, eating disorders can appear bizarre, but are very much a reality in our churches and society today.

Description of Anorexia Nervosa

Anorexia nervosa is an illness characterized by an overwhelming obsession with body weight, with food, and an intense fear of gaining weight. People will adopt bizarre behaviors in order to handle their preoccupation. They will eat smaller portions, refuse to eat at all, and will deny their hunger. They may show an increased interest in food and food planning.[28]

Sufferers will exercise compulsively and excessively, and initially show few signs of fatigue. Some other symptoms are the cessation of menstrual periods for women, which sometimes occurs as weight loss begins; intolerance to cold, especially in hands and feet, as weight loss becomes severe; and the loss of head hair along with growth of fine body and facial hair.[29]

Psychologically, people with anorexia think that they have everything under control as long as they are losing weight, maintaining very little food intake, and adhering to a strict exercise regimen. Appearing to eat normally while not doing so appears to be a common goal, especially among teenage girls. They want to alleviate any questions from parents or friends.

If left untreated, people with this illness develop an emaciated appearance. The body will be so starved for essential nutrients and electrolytes that it will begin to shut down, and a life-threatening illness will develop. This will not happen overnight, but it will happen eventually if not treated medically along with professional counseling.

Description of Bulimia Nervosa

A person can transition from anorexia (starving oneself) to bulimia, which includes bouts of bingeing and purging. Personally, after attempting to eat normally, I would feel bloated and nauseous. My body no longer knew what a "normal" full feeling was. I would crave sweets and eat large quantities of cookies and ice cream. This not only caused me physical discomfort, it caused me to feel extreme guilt over my lack of control. As a result, I began forced vomiting, which gave me immense relief from the uncomfortable, bloated feeling. This allowed me to replace the guilt with a strange calm. As time passed, I settled into a cycle of bingeing and purging, which began to happen more and more frequently. This is not to say that everyone's experience is exactly the same, but there are common generalities among them all.

Sometimes people will abuse laxatives in order to purge. This provides the person with relief from the bloated feeling after bingeing and helps them regain a sense of control.

Finally, a person with bulimia may have a normal weight; however, his or her means of weight control is potentially dangerous. As with anorexia, bulimia must be treated medically along with professional counseling.

Effects on the Family

The word *control* is a common word found among the eating disorders. "Control" is usually at the core of the person's struggle to function and to handle day-to-day activities. Many times parents, siblings, and friends are not aware that their loved one has an eating disorder because that person has done a good job controlling the situation in unnoticeable ways. By the time someone notices the disorder, intervention is critical. Oftentimes, a significant battle begins as the family attempts to force the victim of the illness to give up the symptoms of the disease by using threats, criticism, and punishment.[30] The result is that the entire family struggles along with the person with the disorder. The parents feel guilt and a wide range of emotions as they try to understand why they did not detect the disorder earlier and as they try to learn about the disorder and how to treat it. After treatment starts, it becomes a "three steps forward, two steps back" process. Support is absolutely critical for the family.

Do people overcome an eating disorder? If so, how long does it take? There is no set end result or time frame. Each person's case is individual, and each family's dynamics are unique. No matter what the scenario, medical treatment and professional counseling are necessary along with support for the family from their church. If possible, in situations where the sufferer is a young person, the support of other parents of children with eating disorders can be helpful.

Ministry Strategy

What do you do if you know of someone with an eating disorder, especially if that person does not want to acknowledge the problem? How do you minister to a person with this disorder?

Be Informed

Research and gather as much information as you can on the problem. You do not have to become an expert on the subject, but it helps you to understand the dynamics of eating disorders. There are many resources out there on the Web and in bookstores.

You should also come prepared with a counselor's name for referral, in case the person is ready to get help. You can call the various associations for eating disorders that provide referral services, and seek the names and addresses of effective therapists and treatment programs. Your pastor can also be a resource for names.

Approaching

When you suspect someone is engaging in harmful eating behaviors, you have a responsibility to approach the individual. This is the first step, but it must be done delicately. Remember the person with the eating disorder has done everything secretly.

Here are some dos and don'ts.

1. Do not approach the person publicly. You need to do it privately.

2. Do not make light of what he or she is doing. This is very serious.

3. Do not condemn or criticize the person. That will turn him or her away.

4. Do not give up on the person.

5. Do love him or her.

6. Do show grace and mercy.

7. Do pray before you approach the person.

After taking the time and energy to gather information, you can approach the person with the eating disorder. Express love and concern, not criticism. This is a painful illness, and the first encounter may not be successful. Remember to be patient; it may take multiple encounters.

Here is an example of how you might approach someone:

> Susie, I am concerned about your health because it appears you are losing a great deal of weight. Is everything okay? Are there any health problems? Can I do anything to help you?

The person will respond in one of two ways to your approaching her or him.

Denial

It is not uncommon for the person with an eating disorder to deny she or he has a problem. Secrecy is the sufferer's best friend. The person may be defensive or become angry. They may attack you for even lovingly asking them about it.

You cannot make the person acknowledge a problem. Do not become confrontational or belligerent with the individual because that will only push her or him away. Leave the door open by telling the person that she or he can call you anytime. Tell the individual you will be praying for her or him.

If your suspicions are very strong, you may want to go to your senior pastor or youth pastor and share your concern. If you have firsthand knowledge of the person's behavior, you need to consult with a pastor or a professional to ask how to proceed. If it is a young person, the parents need to know. Because the issue is often a result of family dynamics, telling the parents can exacerbate the problem. Take your senior pastor or youth pastor with you to tell the parents.

Acknowledgment

The willingness to acknowledge the problem is a huge step. Once the sufferer admits to having an eating disorder, there are several things you should do.

Get the person to see an appropriate professional such as a counselor, a pastor, or a medical doctor. Be willing to accompany him or her at least to the first visit. Some people are more willing to go if someone goes with him or her for the first visit.

Stay in a relationship with the individual. Relationships are critically important for the person with an eating disorder. Continue to support and encourage the individual because the road to recovery is difficult.

Help the sufferer focus on God. The eating disorder becomes an idol replacing God in the person's life. Encourage him or her to get into the Word and to pray.

Pray for and with the individual for the following:

1. Courage to deal with the disorder

2. Contentment

3. Willingness to receive God's love and forgiveness

4. For God to reveal the issues contributing to the eating disorder, such as distorted self-image or perfectionism

5. Discovery of who he or she is in Christ (Eph. 1:3–23)

Scripture

Do not condemn: Matthew 7:1; John 3:17; 8:11

We are God's creation: Psalm 139:13–16; Colossians 1:16; 1 Timothy 4:4

God loves: Psalm 118:1–5; John 3:16; 15:9–13

Christians' bodies are God's temple: 1 Corinthians 3:16; 6:19; 2 Corinthians 6:16

God forgives: 2 Chronicles 7:14; Psalm 19:12; Acts 10:43

God heals: Isaiah 53:5; Matthew 9:22; 14:36; 1 Peter 2:2

God's Will
David Wheeler

[11] For I know the thoughts that I think toward you, says the LORD, thoughts of peace and not of evil, to give you a future and a hope.

—Jeremiah 29:11

Overview

Knowing and understanding God's will and plan for one's life can be a difficult proposition at best. Multiple volumes of literature have been dedicated to the subject. Still, many Christians struggle to understand why they exist and exactly what purpose God has in store for them today and in the future. While not exhaustive, the following chapter is designed to shed some light on this essential but elusive topic as you help people who come to you seeking God's will for their lives.

What Is God's Ultimate Will for Man?

[26] Then God said, "Let Us make man in Our image, according to Our likeness; let them have dominion over the fish of the sea, over the birds of the air, and over the cattle, over all the earth and over every creeping thing that creeps on the earth." [27] So God created man in His own image; in the image of God He created him; male and female He created them. [28] Then God

blessed them, and God said to them, "Be fruitful and multiply; fill the earth and subdue it; have dominion over the fish of the sea, over the birds of the air, and over every living thing that moves on the earth."

[29] And God said, "See, I have given you every herb that yields seed which is on the face of all the earth, and every tree whose fruit yields seed; to you it shall be for food. [30] Also, to every beast of the earth, to every bird of the air, and to everything that creeps on the earth, in which there is life, I have given every green herb for food"; and it was so. [31] Then God saw everything that He had made, and indeed it was very good. So the evening and the morning were the sixth day. (Gen. 1:26–31)

In the above passage of Scripture from Genesis 1, it is obvious that from the beginning God created man for a special and intimate relationship with Him. Note what He says in verse 27, "So God created man in His own image; in the image of God He created him; male and female He created them." The very fact that man is created in "His own image" denotes a unique calling for man. Otherwise, why were the animals and trees not created in God's image? The truth is, from the beginning of time, God reserved this special distinction for mankind.

What does this mean for the Christian? And how does this shed light on the subject of knowing and understanding God's personal will for an individual's life? The correct answer is very simple and has two parts:

1. God ultimately created man to glorify His name.

2. After the fall from sin, man's purpose also includes making Him known among the nations.

The Christian's ultimate purpose always is to glorify and exalt God in all he or she does. Therefore the first question you ask the inquirer is "Are you truly glorifying God by your present actions and desires?" If the obvious answer is no, then the person has already answered his or her question.

After determining if the person's actions are exalting God, the next question must be "Is what you are doing advancing God's kingdom and making Him known among the unsaved nations both at home and across the world?" Encourage the person to pray about this. If the person's honest answer is no, then he or she must conclude that the direction of his or her life is not in line with God's eternal purpose.

Think about it, if God was so careful and specific when He created man and the world, His nature has not changed. Everything was created with a purpose to fulfill His ultimate desire to be glorified. In a fallen world, this also includes joining God on His redemptive mission to proclaim His message of salvation to every tribe and nation.

Common Misconceptions Pertaining to Finding God's Will

Like anything else, there are always misconceptions related to the process of discovering God's will in a person's life. The following suggestions are more commonsense than earth-shattering revelations.

One must remember that discovering God's will for one's life is not meant to be a mystical or hidden pursuit. It is sadly amusing to visit a Christian bookstore and peruse the section reserved for books dealing with "finding God's will" in a busy world. Some authors suggest a list of magical surveys and tests aimed at finding the Holy Grail (God's will). The truth is, while some of these approaches can be helpful and even insightful, the bottom line is that since the person is seeking God's will, maybe he or she should begin by addressing Him first. God welcomes people who genuinely "seek" after Him (Matt. 7:7).

One must remember that finding God's will for one's life is not a pursuit only reserved for the professional or full-time clergy. Unfortunately, one of the great lies of the contemporary church is the concept that separates the "clergy" from the "laity." Rest assured, Jesus never meant for His church to outsource the Great Commission to professionals and to miss the perspective that He has an "on-mission" call and will for all Christians.

One must remember that finding God's will for one's life can never contradict His righteous nature. God hates sin. Regardless of the transgression, this truth about sin has never changed, and it never will. For instance, if an individual is seeking God's will about the person to marry, while in an illicit relationship with that same person, do not ask God to legitimatize the sin. It is impossible for God to contradict His sinless nature.

One must remember that finding God's will for one's life is always meant to exalt Him, not the individual. While it is true that discovering God's will enhances the quality of a person's life, always keep in mind the prayer of Jesus in Luke 22:42, "not My will, but Yours, be done." As mentioned earlier, the believer's eternal and universal purpose is to glorify God in all he or she does.

One must remember that finding God's will for one's life does not necessarily lead to a road of comfort and ease. All one has to do is read the New Testament, especially the epistles of Paul, to recognize that following God's will may result in the opposite outcome of comfort and ease. This is noted by the numerous times that Paul was beaten and thrown into prison, all in the name of proclaiming Christ. Yet, as he states in Philippians 1:20–21, "with all boldness, as always, so now also Christ will be magnified in my body, whether by life or by death. For to me, to live is Christ, and to die is gain."

Ministry Strategy

So how do you help the person who comes to you inquiring how to know God's will? Begin by congratulating the inquirer for desiring to know God's will. This is a huge step in glorifying God in his or her life.

Here are seven simple suggestions you can share with the inquirer that will help him or her discover God's will.

1. Make sure that you have a relationship with Jesus Christ. This may sound too obvious to even mention, but knowing Christ in a personal way is always the first and most important aspect in discovering God's will for the Christian's life. Encourage the person to spend a few moments searching his or her soul to make sure that he or she has totally surrendered his or her life under the Lordship of Jesus Christ. The person cannot expect to understand what it means to discover and to follow God's will if his or her life is not surrendered to the Lordship of Jesus Christ.

2. Put yourself into a position of recognizing God's will by walking with Him daily. At this point, it might behoove one to be reminded of Jesus' request that He made to His disciples to tarry with Him in prayer the night before His crucifixion. As you may recall, the disciples repeatedly fell asleep. The result was the scattering of the disciples the next day, while Christ faced the ultimate price on the cross for the sin of mankind.

3. Learn what it means to pray for "His will to be done" in your life. A great example of this occurs in John 4 as the disciples are frantically

trying to get Jesus out of Samaria because of their extreme hatred and prejudice. Jesus ignores the disciples' repeated attempts to feed Him by responding in verse 34, "My food is to do the will of Him who sent Me, and to finish His work." He further states in verse 35, "Do you not say, 'There are still four months and then comes the harvest'? Behold, I say to you, lift up your eyes and look at the fields, for they are already white for harvest!"

4. Practice a life of genuine faith. This is easily summed up in Hebrews 11:6: "But without faith it is impossible to please Him, for he who comes to God must believe that He is, and that He is a rewarder of those who diligently seek Him." Help the inquirer to see the importance of trusting God.

5. Be sensitive to the evidence and confirmation of the Scriptures. This is easily explained by a simple overview of the first several chapters of Acts where Peter and the apostles utilize biblical stories and multiple references to Holy Scripture to support the movement of the Holy Spirit, the birth of the church, and the exclusivity of Christ for eternal salvation. On a personal note, God has never moved in my life to affirm His will without first confirming it through His Holy Word. God primarily uses His Word and He never contradicts His Word.

6. Be accountable and learn to listen to wise counsel. Proverbs 15:22 (MSG), "Refuse good advice and watch your plans fail; take good counsel and watch them succeed." "Good counsel" is the result of wise mentors. Arrogance keeps a person from seeking the insights of others, leading one to make a poor decision. Finding God's will often involves the wisdom of trusted Christian advisors. Wise counsel often comes from the church. What does the church say on the issue?

7. Learn to recognize when and where God is working, then join Him. This is a concept that was made popular through the teachings of Dr. Henry Blackaby in the study *Experiencing God*. Rather than asking God to change His plans to meet your demands, it makes much more biblical sense to acknowledge when and where God is at work, then adjust your life and desires to obediently join Him.

Scripture

1 Samuel 15:22; Psalms 37:3, 5; 40:8; 143:10; Proverbs 3:5–6; Matthew 6:10; John 7:17; Romans 12:1–2; 1 Thessalonians 4:3

Grief
Kent Spann

[36] Then Jesus came with them to a place called Gethsemane, and said to the disciples, "Sit here while I go and pray over there." [37] And He took with Him Peter and the two sons of Zebedee, and He began to be sorrowful and deeply distressed. [38] Then He said to them, "My soul is exceedingly sorrowful, even to death. Stay here and watch with Me."

—Matthew 26:36–38

Overview

Grief is a universal human experience. It is an inevitable human experience. Alfred, Lord Tennyson, the great British poet, wrote a poem titled *In Memoriam* (1850) about grief, doubt, and the search for faith. He wrote:

One writes, that 'Other friends remain,'
    That 'Loss is common to the race'—
    And common is the commonplace,
And vacant chaff well meant for grain.

That loss is common would not make
    My own less bitter, rather more:
    Too common! Never morning wore
To evening, but some heart did break.

Not a day passes that someone does not experience some type of grief.

The Bible is full of accounts of people both righteous and unrighteous who experienced deep grief. David, the man after God's own heart, experienced great grief in his life. He experienced the agonizing grief of losing children (2 Sam. 12:15–18; 13:37; 18:33) as well as the loss of a best friend and a king (2 Sam. 1:17–27). He even suffered the grief of betrayal by a best friend (Ps. 55:12–14). Certainly you cannot talk about grief in the Bible without mentioning Job. There are also accounts of national grief such as when Israel mourned the death of Moses (Deut. 34:8). The Jewish people understood the importance of grieving, which is why they would often grieve forty days. In modern society you are expected to be back to normal routine in a week.

Even Jesus the perfect man was not immune to the pain of grief. In Isaiah 53:3, Jesus is called the "Man of sorrows." The Hebrew word translated "sorrows" (mak'ovot) speaks of a deep mental anguish. He is also described in that passage as "a Man ... acquainted with grief." The word *grief* is variously translated "disease," "affliction," "sadness," and "grief." This word closely connects the emotional grief with sickness or physical suffering, which is very insightful. Grieving does affect a person emotionally but it also affects the person physically. The same word is used later in Isaiah 53:10 where God is described as putting Him to grief. But not only did Jesus feel his sorrow (Isa. 53:3), He also bore or felt our sorrow (Isa. 53:4).

Later in the Gospels we see Jesus the man of grief. In Mark 3:5 Jesus is grieved by the hardness of the religious leaders' hearts. The most revealing event, however, is Jesus in the Garden of Gethsemane where He is filled with sorrow and grief as He faced the cross (Matt. 26:36–44; Mark 14:32–42). Luke, the physician, adds an enlightening note that Jesus sweat blood. Herschel Hobbs graphically interprets Luke's account, "With a physician's touch Luke says that his 'sweat was as if it were great drops of blood falling down to the ground.' He broke out into a bloody sweat which became clotted blood."[31] There is a rare medical condition called hematidrosis in which a human being literally sweats blood. The MacArthur Study Bible says this condition "can be caused by extreme anguish or physical strain. Subcutaneous capillaries dilate and burst, mingling blood with sweat. Christ Himself stated that His distress had brought Him to the threshold of death."[32] The point is that Jesus experienced a level of grief that no one else has ever felt.

Grief Defined

Grief is the natural human response to loss. It is a deep and sometimes very intense emotional suffering. Other things may accompany it such as physical issues like fatigue or sickness, and even mental issues such as preoccupation with thoughts of the individual or extreme thoughts like suicide, but at its core it is emotional suffering. It is a sad and lonely state.

Usually we associate grief with the experience of death. The death of a loved one such as a parent or a spouse certainly brings a deep grief. In fact, it has been said that there are few blows to the human spirit as great as the loss of a loved one. Death is the reality of life on this planet, and thus grieving for the death of a loved one is a part of life on this planet.

While grief is certainly the normal response to death, it is also the response to life. Grief occurs anytime there is loss, including living losses. Living losses occur in the course of living life. There is the husband grieving as his wife of twenty years walks out the door for good. Many parents have felt loss as their child disappoints them because of life choices. There is the loss of a dream. It may be the loss of a lifelong dream of a career that is not going to happen now. It is the loss of one's youth. For some it is the loss of one's health due to an injury or a debilitating disease. It may the loss of a job. There can be the loss of a friend who, because of a job transfer, is now living on the other side of the country. The family standing outside their home as it burns to the ground with all their treasured possessions knows true loss. A church feels a sense of loss when their pastor announces that he has accepted the call to another church. The pastor leaving the church that he has loved for so long feels a sense of loss. When a church goes through a painful split, there is loss that means grieving. In all these cases there is a grieving process that takes place because there is loss. Loss brings grief.

There is grieving that takes place when there is death; there is grieving that comes in the losses of life.

The Influences on Grief

No two people grieve exactly alike. While there may be common experiences of grief as we shall see, each case of grief is unique. The person seeking to minister to those in a time of grief needs to be aware of what makes each case unique, so he or she can respond properly. Below are a few things that can influence the extent and even expression of grief.

The extent of grief is influenced by the type of loss. The closer the relationship the griever had with the person who died, the greater the grief. Thus the death of a wife of sixty years is vastly different from the loss of a childhood friend. The grief brought on by a tragic and unexpected, possibly even violent, death is very different from the grief of someone who has watched a loved one die a slow and painful death. The grief caused by the loss of one's physical health (paralysis or multiple sclerosis) is not the same as the loss of a job of thirty years.

The extent of grief is influenced by the background and personality of the individual. Some people are very expressive of their grief, while others hold it in. A person who is very secure and independent will handle grief quite differently from one who is insecure and dependent. A good gauge is how the person handles stress in his or her normal life. Also past experiences of grief can give you insight into how the individual will handle a current situation.

How someone grieves is influenced by the belief system of the individual. This is true whether someone is a Christian or an atheist. While Christians grieve, their grief is quite different as Paul states in 1 Thessalonians 4:13–14:

> [13] But I do not want you to be ignorant, brethren, concerning those who have fallen asleep, lest you sorrow as others who have no hope. [14] For if we believe that Jesus died and rose again, even so God will bring with Him those who sleep in Jesus.

The extent of grief is influenced by the cultural norms, in other words by how one's culture grieves. Someone from China will express grief quite differently from someone from the Middle East. Even within a geographic region there can be multiple cultures.

The Process of Grief

Materials refer to stages of grief or cycles of grief, but grief is more of a process than a stage. The terminology of stages indicates an orderly step-by-step process, which is not always the case. The number of stages varies among different writers. Granger E. Westberg in his book *Good Grief* identifies ten stages:[33]

1. We are in a state of shock.

2. We express emotion.

3. We feel depressed and lonely.

4. We may experience physical symptoms of distress.

5. We may become panicky.

6. We feel a sense of guilt about the loss.

7. We are filled with anger and resentment.

8. We resist returning.

9. Gradually hope comes through.

10. We struggle to affirm reality.

Elisabeth Kübler-Ross formulated the classic process outline of grief in her work *On Death and Dying*. She reduced it to five stages:[34]

1. Denial: The person is in shock or numbed. The individual cannot believe it has really happened.

2. Anger: The person feels anger. He or she may be angry at the doctor, angry at the children for not being there, and even angry at himself or herself. Anger can be directed at the deceased expressed by "Why did they leave me?" Anger at the deceased is especially prevalent when death is by suicide or the result of a foolish choice like drinking while driving. Many times the anger will be directed toward God.

3. Bargaining: This may take the form of questions like "Why Lord?" The griever may move to "If" questions: "If only he did not go on that trip," or "If only I would have been there." The person may even try to bargain with God.

4. Depression: The person feels depressed and lonely. A great sadness settles in on the griever. A dark cloud settles over the person's life. For some it may even turn to despair.

5. Acceptance: The griever begins to accept the loss and hurt. The person begins to look beyond to what is to come.

Again grief is not a neat orderly process but it helps you, the comforter, to understand what is going on in the griever's life. You can also share the processes with the griever, which can be of great help because oftentimes the person may wonder if he or she is the only one who feels this way.

This process can last between one to three years, but no one can set down a hard and fast schedule because every situation as well as griever is unique.

Ministry Strategy

The Scripture is clear on the strategy of ministry to the bereaved and grieving. We are to come alongside those who mourn and weep (John 11:35; Rom. 12:15).

Death

THE CALL. You will receive the call of someone's death in either one of two ways: directly from the bereaved or from another source such as a friend or the church office.

If the call comes from the bereaved there are a few things to do and keep in mind. Listen and pray for God's guidance. Express your condolences. Ask if you may come and visit with her or him. The reason you need to ask is they may not want company presently. If they want a visit, find out the best time and place to visit with them. Sometimes they will be leaving to go to the funeral home, the hospital, or a relative's house. Pray with her or him on the phone if she or he is okay with that, especially if you are not going to be able to visit for a while. Call your church office or pastor to make sure they are aware of the death. Do not assume anyone has contacted the church.

If you find out about a death from a secondary source, be sure to get all information about the deceased if you do not know her or him. It is helpful if you can get family information such as the names of children, parents, or siblings who may be with the bereaved. Inquire if there are any special circumstances you might be unaware of about the situation. The deceased may have died violently, may have been estranged from her or his children, or there may have been family conflicts. Inquire if there is someone from the church staff going to the home. Call the bereaved.

THE VISIT. Take someone with you, especially if you are visiting someone of the opposite sex, and she or he is there alone. Be aware of what is happening when you walk in the door. Is there a crowd of people, or is the person alone? Is the bereaved lying down or moving around? Be sensitive to the person when you arrive. She or he may want to hug you, but she or he may not. She or he may want to talk, or maybe not. Keep your words brief. It is your presence that counts. The best thing Job's friends did was just sit with him (Job 2:11–13). It was when they started talking that they created pain (Job 4–37; 42:7–9). Let the person talk if she or he wants to. Many times she or he will want to recall memories or tell what happened at their loved one's death. Offer practical support such as making phone calls, picking up people at the airport, or making hotel arrangements. Ask if you can read Scripture, and pray with her or him. Oftentimes the bereaved wants to reach out to God at this time but cannot because of the pain. Your comments on Scripture and your prayer should be brief, calling upon God to strengthen and help the person. You may want to give the person a piece of literature or a very small book, such as *Good Grief* by Granger E. Westberg or *Experiencing Grief* by H. Norman Wright, that helps her or him understand grief. Your church may have materials you can give the individual.

There are several things you should avoid. You do not have to say something profound or solve all the person's problems. You should avoid saying, "I know how you feel" because you do not. Every person's pain is unique. Also avoid saying things like "Get hold of yourself" or "It's not as bad as it could be." Do not try to correct the person in her or his grief, which is what Job's friends did. The exception to the rule is if the person is threatening to harm herself or himself or make a big decision that should not be made at that moment. Stay out of family conflicts or negative conversations. Call the church office or your pastor to report on your visit, especially if you received helpful information. Alert appropriate support groups such as small-group leaders, elders, and so on. Attend the viewing and service if possible.

AFTER CARE. Make a series of follow-up visits with the bereaved at key intervals. Visit at one to two weeks. The loneliest times come after all the family and friends have left. At three to four weeks you should visit to let the individual know she or he has not been forgotten. At this point the griever is beginning to ponder the deeper questions such as "Where was God?" or "Why did this happen?" At two to three months, significant issues begin to surface. Contact the bereaved on special anniversaries such as the deceased's birthday, wedding anniversary, and, most important, the one-year anniversary of the person's death. Encourage the person to get into a grief support group. Many churches offer these groups. Keep the pastor updated, especially if you pick up on significant issues. Share the three steps to recovery: grieve the loss; believe God and His promises (Ps. 119; Col. 3:16); receive God's comfort and grace. Continue to pray for the person(s).

Death of a Child

The death of a child, especially an infant, is one of the most painful experiences a person can endure. The pain is different from all other. In addition to the things already covered you need to be aware of some additional things.

THE MARRIAGE. Unlike when one of the marriage partner's parents dies and the other partner can play the role of comforter, when a child dies both are bereaved. The divorce rate is extremely high for a couple who loses a child. This does not mean it is inevitable; it does mean it can happen. As the comforter, you will want to be aware of the state of the marriage. Here are some things to be aware of from the parents:

- Lack of communication.
- Overprotectiveness of the other children.
- Blame and guilt. One parent may blame the other.
- Wondering when, where, and how to deal with a child's belongings.
- Turning away from each other.
- Anger toward each other.
- Realizing that if a couple had problems before the child's death, those problems can become more difficult to deal with now.

THE SIBLINGS. It is easy for the siblings to get lost in the process of ministering to the parents. Make sure they are cared for. There are things you need to be aware of:

- The sibling may feel responsible for the death.
- The sibling may have suicidal thoughts.

- A sibling may feel extreme anger or depression, which can be expressed in very outward ways but also internalized.

THE FAMILY STRUCTURE. The whole family structure is thrown into chaos when a child dies. The father or mother may not be able to function and therefore do the normal things the family has come to expect. Family routines can be severely disrupted or altered.

Death of an Unbeliever

The death of an unbeliever can be one of the most difficult situations for the comforter especially when it is a well-known fact that the deceased was not a believer.

Do not convince the individual that the deceased is in heaven. You do not want to create false hope. Do not pass judgment on the deceased. Focus on the good things about the person while he or she lived. This is especially true in the initial days after death. Do offer hope. No one knows what goes on in the final moments of a person's life. Deathbed conversions are real (Luke 23:39–43). Do not be afraid to discuss what the Bible says if the grieving person brings it up. If you can, you will want to defer this conversation until after the funeral. Do not be afraid to say you do not know. Do share Christ in the days ahead with those who are still living. It is not usually best to try to share in the early days and weeks. Be sensitive to the Holy Spirit and His timing.

Living Losses

A living loss is any loss that does not involve death. Many of the same issues covered under death apply to living losses such as stages of grief and the need for hope. What separates this from the loss in death is the lack of opportunity for closure. When a spouse dies, there can be closure; when the spouse walks out on the marriage the griever still may encounter the other spouse, especially if there are children. The truth is, people do not know how to grieve living losses. Worse yet they are not given permission to grieve the loss of their job, dream, career, church, or health. Here are some steps to help one grieving a living loss:

1. Realize each situation is unique, and thus the nature of grief will vary.

2. Encourage the person to grieve. Show the person why it is important. Help the individual to understand that grieving is God's way of getting through loss.

3. Help the person develop a recovery plan. This is a big part of grieving living losses. What is the person going to do now that he or she cannot work due to a disability? What will he do in the face of a job loss? How can he dream again?

4. Remind the person that God still has a plan for her or his life (Jer. 29:11; Rom. 8:28).

5. Recommend journaling. Journaling is a

lost art in today's culture but is extremely therapeutic. Much of the Old Testament is a journal. It is God's people processing life.

6. Suggest he writes a letter of closure. It may be a letter saying good-bye to a dream or vision. It may be a letter of closure after a divorce. This helps a person to let it go.

7. Be a friend.

8. Pray with the person about her or his real concerns.

The bottom line is the grief is just as real in living losses as in death.

The Good Comforter

1. Be a good listener.

2. Let the person know it is okay to grieve. Ecclesiastes 3:4 says there is a time to weep and mourn.

3. Grieve with the person.

4. Encourage the griever that he or she will get through it. One grieving father said, "You never get over it but you do get through it."

5. Share the Christian hope (Rom. 5:1–5; 1 Thess. 4:13, 18).

6. Do not preach or condemn.

7. Do not be afraid to talk about the person's loss.

8. Do not minimize the person's loss.

9. Do not be afraid to admit you do not know the answers.

Scripture

Jesus understands sorrow: Isaiah 53:3, 4; Matthew 26:36–44; Mark 14:32–42

Jesus intercedes for His child: Hebrews 4:15–16; 7:25

The Holy Spirit comforts: John 14:16–18, 25–27; Acts 9:29–31

God the Father comforts: Isaiah 66:13; 2 Corinthians 1:3–7

Jesus comforts: John 14:1–4; 2 Thessalonians 2:16

The Christian and death: 1 Corinthians 15:35–58; 2 Corinthians 5:1–8; Philippians 1:21–23; 3:20–21; 1 Thessalonians 4:13–18; 2 Timothy 10; 1 Peter 1:3–9

Scriptures that can be shared with those grieving: Psalms 16:11; 20:1, 2; 23:1–6; 25:16–22; 27:4–5; 30:1–5; 34:17–20; 46:1–3; 62:5–8; 91:1–16; 121:1–8; Isaiah 40:1–2, 11, 28–31; 41:10; 43:1–2; Jeremiah 29:11–13; Lamentations 3:22–24; Matthew 5:4; 11:28–30; John 10:27–29; 11:25–26; 14:1–6; Romans 8:28; 31–39; 2 Corinthians 4:16–18; 12:9; 1 Thessalonians 4:13–18; Hebrews 4:14–16; 1 Peter 5:10; Revelation 14:13; 21:1–5

You are encouraged to study each of these passages and add to the list those you find in your own reading.

Hospital Ministry
Kent Spann

[34] "Then the King will say to those on His right hand, 'Come, you blessed of My Father, inherit the kingdom prepared for you from the foundation of the world: [35] for I was hungry and you gave Me food; I was thirsty and you gave Me drink; I was a stranger and you took Me in; [36] I was naked and you clothed Me; I was sick and you visited Me; I was in prison and you came to Me.'

[37] "Then the righteous will answer Him, saying, 'Lord, when did we see You hungry and feed You, or thirsty and give You drink? [38] When did we see You a stranger and take You in, or naked and clothe You? [39] Or when did we see You sick, or in prison, and come to You?' [40] And the King will answer and say to them, 'Assuredly, I say to you, inasmuch as you did it to one of the least of these My brethren, you did it to Me.'"

—Matthew 25:34–40

Overview

Sickness is a part of life on this fallen planet. No one likes sickness whether it is a simple cold or a serious brain tumor. Sickness interrupts our day-to-day routine and, in severe cases, our life plans. This chapter is not an attempt to deal with the "whys" of sickness, rather, it is about ministering to those who are sick. Jesus in Matthew 25:34–40 did not give an explanation for sickness; He did speak to the importance of ministering to those who are sick.

Hospital visitation is a very important part of caring for those who are sick. According to the American Hospital Association, in 2008 there were 37,529,270 admissions to registered hospitals. Each of those 37 million-plus people represents someone with real needs, not only physically but spiritually, emotionally, and mentally.

What is the purpose of hospital visitation? There are many purposes. Here are just a few:

1. To be an ambassador for Christ. Jesus said that we are His ambassadors when we visit the sick and afflicted (Matt. 25:34–36).

2. To show the compassion and love of Christ to the hurting and suffering.

3. To offer encouragement to those who may be afraid, discouraged, lonely, and uncertain.

4. To affirm the members of the family. The family members often suffer too as they watch their loved one in pain or distress.

5. To show friendship to the sick.

6. To let the person who is sick, as well as the family, know that there is a group of people who sincerely care about them.

7. To encourage the person through Scripture and prayer.

8. To share Christ when it is appropriate.

Ministry Strategy

Preparing for the Hospital Visit

Preparing properly for the visit you are making is very important. It can be the difference between a meaningful visit and a regrettable visit. A series of questions will help the hospital visitor properly prepare for the visit.

1. Where am I going? Am I going to a hospital, a rehabilitation center, a specialty facility? Is the person in the emergency room or a regular room?

2. Who am I visiting? Know as much as you can about the person you are visiting so the visit will be more effective.

   a. Is the patient a Christian? If not, is he or she receptive to a visit from you as a representative of the church?

   b. Is the patient a member of the church? Is one of the family members a member of the church?

   c. Who is the patient's family?

   d. What is the patient's condition? Why is the person in the hospital or convalescent center?

3. Why am I making the visit?

    a. Does the patient want or need a visit? Did he or she request a visit?

    b. Is the visit a social or ministry visit?

4. Do I need to call the patient before visiting?

5. Is the person having surgery? If yes, when?

6. What are the hospital regulations and rules?

    a. When are the visiting hours?

    b. Will you be able to see the patient? He or she may be in isolation or intensive care where you cannot visit. In those cases you will want to make sure a family member is present if you go.

7. If you cannot visit, are there alternatives, such as making a phone call, sending a letter or card, assisting the family at home, and so on?

8. Does the pastor know that this patient is in the hospital? Do not assume your pastor knows because many times he does not.

Making the Hospital Visit

Before entering the patient's room, wash your hands thoroughly. Watch for signs that say: "Isolation," "No Visitors," "Oxygen in Use," or for lights flashing over the door. These signs are there for your safety as well as for the patient's. If you are uncertain about the meaning of the sign, go to the nurses' station and ask. Knock before entering. If there is no response, go to the nurses' station to get permission to enter the room. Never push a door completely open until the patient gives you permission to come in the room. Do not awaken the patient unless the patient told you to awaken him or her. Sleep is a very important part of a patient's recovery. Do leave a note that you were there and include the time and date. Consider what passage of Scripture you are going to share with the patient. It is best to mark it in advance so you can quickly turn to the verses you want to read. Use a small pocket Bible because a large Bible may be overwhelming. Sometimes the room will have a Gideon Bible, but do not count on that.

Upon entering the patient's room, size up the situation when you walk in. What is the patient doing? Is the patient in obvious severe pain? Does he or she seem happy or depressed? Is the patient or a family member upset (perhaps he or she just received distressing news)? Are there medical personnel in the room? Do not react to what you may see. The patient can pick up on that. Do not make comments about what you see. Introduce yourself clearly and distinctly.

Let the patient lead in shaking your hand because there may be a physical condition preventing him or her from doing so. Consider where you stand or sit. Notice where equipment is located, where windows are (the glare can hurt the patient's eyes), where family members are, the elevation of the patient's bed, and so forth so that the patient does not have to strain in order to communicate with you. Let the patient lead the conversation. He or she may not want to start off talking about the illness. Let the person choose the course of the conversation. If the patient does not lead in conversation, try asking, "How are things going?" Avoid asking, "How do you feel?" or "What is wrong with you?"

Before leaving, ask if you can read Scripture and have prayer with the person. This is important because in that moment you are God's representative to that individual. He or she needs a Word from God. (See suggested verses in the next section.) If you are visiting a child, ask for the parent's permission to read Scripture and pray. If the patient is comatose, ask the family member if you can pray with the patient. Read Scripture and pray as though the comatose patient can hear you. Leave your name and phone number so the patient has the option to contact you.

After your visit wash your hands to avoid spreading germs. The patient may not have a contagious disease but the hospital is a place where sick people are. I picked up a staph infection while visiting someone in a rehabilitation center. Report your visit to your local church. Be sure to share relevant information. Pray for the person you visited.

The Dos and Don'ts of the Hospital Visit

1. Do be cheerful.

2. Do be a good listener.

3. Do be considerate of other patients in the room.

4. Do acknowledge other patients in the room but be sensitive; the roommate may not want to talk.

5. Do not be loud.

6. Do not be in a hurry, but do not stay too long. Some rules of thumb:

   a. A person you do not know: ten minutes or less.

   b. A person in intensive care: five minutes or less.

   c. A person you know and who is fully alert: no more than thirty minutes.

   d. Of course the bottom line is to ascertain the patient's need or desire. He or she may want you to stay longer or shorter. Be sensitive.

7. Do not be afraid of silence. Make the visit brief and leave.

8. Do not offer false optimism nor create pessimism.

9. Do not try to second-guess the doctor.

10. Do not get drawn into criticism of doctors, family members, or others.

11. Do not get in the way of medical personnel.

12. Do not sit on the bed.

13. Do not give patients anything to eat or drink or any medication unless you know it is okay for them to have it. Sometimes the patient will ask you for something that he or she is not allowed to receive. This is especially true of food and drink.

14. Do not visit if you are sick.

15. Do not discuss the "sleeping" or comatose patient's condition with family members while in the room. The patient may not be sleeping, and many times comatose patients do hear what is being said in the room, so it is better to go outside the room if discussions are necessary.

16. When visiting someone who has had a baby, do not speak to the mother and father about the baby unless you know the baby is living and well. Let them tell you what is going on.

17. Do not reveal anything you know about the patient and his or her condition. The patient may not know what you know.

18. Do not assume anything.

Privacy and Confidentiality

If you have been to a doctor's office recently you have signed HIPAA documents. HIPAA stands for Health Insurance Portability and Accountability Act of 1996. It was passed to ensure insurance coverage could be kept as a person moved from one employer to another as well as to protect the privacy rights of the patient. Because of HIPAA, hospital personnel are very limited in what they can tell you. You need to be aware of and sensitive to the issues of privacy and confidentiality. Ask permission to share what you learn.

Scripture

Affliction: Psalm 55:22; Romans 5:3–5; 2 Corinthians 4:16–18; Hebrews 12:10–11

Awaiting a Biopsy/Test Result: Psalm 139:1–6, 9–12, 17, 18; Isaiah 40:31; Matthew 6:30–34

Birth of a Child: 1 Samuel 1:19, 20, 24, 26–28; Psalms 127; 128

Facing Surgery: Psalms 17:6–8; 27:1; 91:11; 103:1–4, 8–12; 121:1–8; Romans 8:31–39; 1 John 4:9–10

Little Hope for Recovery/Bad News: Psalms 23; 86:1–7; Isaiah 35:10; John 10:27–28

Long Convalescence: Psalms 4; 43:1–15; 77:1–15; 138; John 15:1–17; Romans 12; Hebrews 11

Permanent Injury: Psalms 57:1–3; 118:4–6; Isaiah 40:28–31; 41:10; 49:14–16; Romans 8:26–28, 39

Serious Accident: Psalms 91:1, 2, 11–16; 116:1–4; Romans 5:1–5

Mental Disorders
James L. Smith

¹²Now David took these words to heart, and was very much afraid of Achish the king of Gath. ¹³So he changed his behavior before them, pretended madness in their hands, scratched on the doors of the gate, and let his saliva fall down on his beard. ¹⁴Then Achish said to his servants, "Look, you see the man is insane. Why have you brought him to me?"

—1 Samuel 21:12–14

Overview

Mental Disorders and the Bible

Even in King David's day, a distinction was made between mental illness and demon possession. David acted odd in order to be ignored by his enemies. Today, too many people in the church do not know how to interact with the mentally ill; or, like Achish, they do not want to be bothered with them.

Christians are not immune to mental disorders. Some fear being judged as weak in their faith because of having psychological and emotional disorders. The truth is that just as some strong Christians live with chronic health problems like diabetes or respiratory problems, others live with mental disorders. For lay ministers, the issue becomes how do we provide care as Christian witnesses while walking alongside those who struggle with mental disorders?

According to statistics from the U.S. Department of Health, 9.8 million adults (4.4 percent) had a diagnosable mental health disorder in the year 2008, not including alcohol and other drug disorders.[35] This means that in a church of 100 members, 4 or 5 parishioners are affected. In the large churches, for every 1,000 people who attend, 44 or 45 people are affected.

Mental Disorders

Because of the large number of disorders listed in the *Diagnostic and Statistical Manual of Mental Disorders* (*DSM-IV*), the scope of this chapter will be primarily on pastoral care skills rather than specific disorders. For those seeking detailed information on a particular disorder, the National Institute of Mental Health Internet Web site is an excellent resource.

Causes of Mental Illness

Several factors can contribute to the disorders, including adverse reactions to medications; alcohol and other drugs; trauma and significant losses; cumulative stressors that push people beyond their coping skills; head injuries from accidents, infections, strokes, or high fevers; or genetic predispositions.

There are several symptoms to be aware of:

1. Significant behavioral changes such as appearance

2. Isolation

3. Confusion

4. Extreme mood swings such as agitation, deep sadness, or euphoria

5. Inappropriate moods such as showing no feelings during a crisis or unusual happiness immediately after a period of deep depression

6. Delusions: false beliefs such as claiming to be royalty or believing that the FBI is after him or her

7. Hallucinations: reports of seeing, hearing, smelling, tasting, or feeling things that do not exist, such as giant spiders or voices that tell the person to commit suicide

Acute and Chronic Disorders

Types of disorders can be broken down into acute and chronic disorders. People with an acute disorder have a rapid onset of symptoms. Those who live with chronic disorders may not remember a time when they did not have the symptoms.

Treatments, including medical and counseling interventions that do not require hospitalization, are available for most disorders. Short-term hospitalization sometimes may be appropriate, especially as medications are adjusted. Surprisingly, many who are hospitalized report afterward that they felt safe and protected from the demands of the world at a critical time.

Ministry Strategy

Nonemergency Care

Families often seek prayer, support, and direction during mental disorder situations. These opportunities are similar to visiting a family with physical health problems.

1. Use active listening skills.

2. Reassure them of God's unconditional love.

3. Encourage them to utilize medical and counseling resources.

4. Advise those who have questions about treatment to directly ask their physicians and counselors.

Unexpected Encounters

Occasionally, providers are confronted with crises without any warning. The following case studies are fictitious. They are created as examples of potential problems to stimulate thinking. Note that the level of urgency in each case varies greatly.

A member has never used any type of medication, including aspirin. He returns home following his first surgery and is recovering well. As you visit his home, he whispers in your ear that the Mafia has been watching his house ever since he returned from the hospital.

Late one evening, Bob is praying loudly and irrationally in the church sanctuary. He laughs inappropriately saying that the Holy Spirit filled him with a special anointing. His concerned spouse is with him and wants to know if this is truly God manifesting Himself in Bob.

The church organist, who has played for your church for many years, comes to you after a service and says that she cannot travel to Bermuda to play for a specific wedding. Her comment is unusual. You tell a relative about what was said. The relative dismisses it. Six months later, the organist is trying frantically to unlock her car in the parking lot, but it is not her vehicle and does not resemble the one that she drives.

A middle-aged man who comes from a family that has a history of several psychiatric disorders has just been released from a psychiatric care unit after a week of treatment. He had believed for years that God had spared him because of his faith in Jesus Christ. He is discouraged and questions not only the depth of his faith but also the goodness of God.

Eve, who attends church regularly, calls to thank you for your help as a lay minister. She then tells you that Satan has told her to kill herself.

Triage

Triage is the process of prioritizing elements of crises at hand. It is a time to determine what must occur first and what can wait until later.

You must also determine if you should even be there. There is a time and place for pastoral intervention. Risks need to be factored into the equation. Lay ministers are not police officers or paramedics. If a person is a threat to self or others, other professionals need to intervene first. Unlike the hero in the movies who crawls onto a ledge with a suicidal jumper to persuade the jumper not to act, lay ministers do not naively take chances while boldly stating God will protect him or her from harm. Remember that Satan told Jesus that if He were to throw Himself down from the highest point of the temple that angels would save him. Jesus responded by saying, "It is written again, 'You shall not tempt the LORD your God'" (Matt. 4:7).

There are questions to help you determine when immediate intervention is necessary:

- Is the person a threat to self or others? If you are at risk, exit the building, then contact 911 or law enforcement agencies immediately.
- Does the person recognize you? If not, seek help from friends, families, and neighbors. If no one is available, contact 911 or a local hospital and explain the situation.
- Is the person receptive to your presence and able to respond to instructions or questions? If not, exit the home and make necessary phone calls at another location.

Ministry Considerations

Respect the person's space. She or he may not want to be touched, not even for prayer. Always be calm. If you are calm, many will find strength and comfort in this. Express your concern for the person.

Do not address spiritual needs if the person is confused or irrational. This may not be the time to share Scripture verses. If the person is open to prayer or wants to discuss the Bible, this may be appropriate if it does not increase the person's symptoms.

Utilize support. Are there caring relatives, friends, or neighbors who can assist now? Can this support person make a call to a physician, counselor, or hospital emergency room?

Do not make promises that you cannot keep. Do not offer to "keep a secret." The secret may include a suicide plan or something that needs to be reported, such as child abuse. The goal is to connect the parishioner to professional care. Your pastor can give you names of competent Christian counselors.

Medications are frequently needed to treat certain mental disorders. Some Christians have the attitude that if a person truly had faith, medications would not be necessary. When such views are expressed to the one with the disorder, this creates guilt and shame. A broader theology needs to be offered. Note that Paul's close friend in his missionary journeys was Luke, the physician. There is no record of Paul discrediting Luke's work. God has placed us in an era in which medications are available for healing. God expects us to use these resources.

If the individual cannot afford medications, many pharmaceutical companies are willing to assist those who lack funds to purchase needed medications. The lay minister can assist by making an inquiry to the company to find out the appropriate steps.

Encourage the individual to follow the directions of the doctors. Also encourage the individual to seek help immediately if there are possible problems related to the medications. Reassure the person that the use of medications does not indicate a lack of faith.

Strengthening the Mental Health Care of the Church

Approach the pastoral staff and appropriate church leaders or committees to discuss ways to address mental health concerns in the church. Here are suggestions:

- Offer training events for lay ministers and interested persons.
- Include information on specific disorders, such as depression, in the church newsletter.
- Educate the membership through pamphlets, special speakers, and appropriate books in the church library.
- Post mental health emergency numbers on church bulletin boards.
- Locate Christian therapists who integrate faith and therapy.
- Obtain information from mental health resources before situations occur.

Remember that your presence as a Christian helper incarnates God's love for the wounded.

Scripture

Fear: Psalms 27:1; 32:7; Philippians 4:6–7; 1 John 4:18
Sadness: Matthew 5:4; John 14:1
Hope: Psalm 30:5; John 14:16, 18
God's Love: John 15:9; Romans 5:8; 1 John 4:19
Strength: Psalm 27:14; Isaiah 41:10; Philippians 4:13

Resources

American Association of Christian Counselors (AACC). AACC provides a number of resources, including the names of Christian therapists, books, and training. See http://www.aacc.net.

Focus on the Family. This Web site has numerous resources from a Christian perspective. See http://www.focusonthefamily.com.

The National Institute of Mental Health. See http://www.nimh.nih.gov/index.shtml.

Substance Abuse and Mental Health Administration Services (SAMHSA). Search online at http://www.samhsa.gov. Information, including free pamphlets, is available simply by asking.

Ministering to Your Minister
Fred Milacci

[16] The Lord grant mercy to the household of
Onesiphorus, for he often refreshed me [Paul],
and was not ashamed of my chain; [17] but when he
arrived in Rome, he sought me out very zealously
and found me. [18] The Lord grant to him that he may
find mercy from the Lord in that Day—and you
know very well how many ways he ministered to
me at Ephesus.

—2 Timothy 1:16–18

Overview

Pop quiz: Whose job do you think it is to care for
and minister to people in the church who are hurting
or in need? If you answered, "the pastor's," no doubt you
would be in agreement with just about everyone who
would respond to this question. And to be honest, it is
really not a stretch to say that it is the pastor's job to meet
the needs of those in the congregation, especially when
you consider that the word *pastor* means "to shepherd,"
and that, according to the apostle Peter, pastors are to
guide and guard the flock of God (i.e., the church, see
1 Peter 5:1–4).

Okay, so it is clear that people in need should expect
to be ministered to by, well, the minister (by the way,
"minister" is a fancy word for servant). But equally

true—and perhaps even more important to remember—
is that pastors are people too, with marriages, family
problems, mortgages, car troubles, aches and pains, and
needs of their own. What is more, because the pastor is,
in the end, just a person, we need to realize that he is just
as susceptible to the same kinds of temptations; his faith
is not any more automatic, and it is no easier for him to
be a loving, kind, hopeful person than it is for anyone
else.[36]

It is bad enough that people in the pew are prone to
forget (or overlook) that pastors are human. Even worse,
however, is when they buy into some of the common
misconceptions about pastoral ministry such as pastors
only work one day a week, should put the needs of the
church over their own families, do not need any privacy
or time off, or are made of Teflon and do not feel pain.

It is that last misconception—or better, myth—that
is perhaps most cutting to and problematic for pastors
and their families, especially in light of the following
statistics:

- 90 percent of those in the pastorate report
  working fifty-five to seventy-five hours a week
- 70 percent feel they are grossly underpaid
- 80 percent of pastors believe their work has
  negatively affected their families
- 90 percent feel they are inadequately trained to
  cope with their job's demands
- 50 percent of pastors feel unable to meet the
  demands of their jobs

- 70 percent of those in this pastoral ministry constantly fight depression
- 70 percent of pastors do not have someone they consider a close friend
- 50 percent feel so discouraged that they would leave their jobs if they could, but have no other way of making a living
- 80 percent of pastors' wives wish their husbands would choose a different profession

In fact, this same study revealed that the pastorate is rated near the bottom of a list of the most-respected professions, just above "car salesman." It should not surprise us, then, that every month, on average, 1,700 pastors leave the ministry with an additional 1,300 being terminated by their local church, often without cause.[37]

All of this raises the question: who then should minister to the minister? The short answer is simply you, me, all of us; we are all called to support, encourage, and minister to pastors and their families. As Aaron and Hur did for Moses when his "hands became heavy" (Ex. 17:12) during a battle, it is our job to stand alongside and support God's man. How we go about doing this is what we will explore in the rest of this chapter.

Ministry Strategy

The apostle Paul was perhaps the greatest pastor, church planter, missionary, evangelist, and minister of the gospel to have ever lived. But coupled with his great ministry success was an even greater amount of personal suffering that included being savagely beaten many times, arrested, wrongfully imprisoned, shipwrecked, and experiencing any number of physical, emotional, and spiritual perils (see 2 Cor. 11:23–28). And he experienced all of this on top of what he referred to as his daily and "deep concern for all the churches" (2 Cor. 11:28), which he loved and ministered to. And though he "[took] pleasure" in enduring all of these problems "for Christ's sake" (2 Cor. 12:10), that does not mean he did not get down, discouraged, feel overwhelmed, or pray desperately for relief from his troubles; after all, he was just a man.

That is where Paul's friends came in, one of which was a man named Onesiphorus. Aside from the fact that his name means "profit-bearing,"[38] we really do not know much about Onesiphorus, only that he had a long-term, intentional, and profitable (for Paul) ministry that was focused on meeting the apostle's needs any way he could (see 2 Tim. 1:18), especially—but not exclusively—when Paul was hurting. In his second letter to Timothy, Paul shares how Onesiphorus helped and served him while Paul was in prison; what Onesiphorus did for Paul is instructive for those of us who wish to minister to pastors today.

For one thing, Onesiphorus was, for Paul, refreshing, a breath of fresh air. Onesiphorus was one of those rare individuals whose very presence was, to others, like a cool breeze on a hot, muggy day: inviting, refreshing, invigorating. He was the kind of person you wanted to be around, and wanted to be around you, especially if you are in ministry and struggling. These people can be characterized as uplifting, encouraging, and a bright spot even on the darkest day; they seem to have a knack for saying and doing the right thing at the right time; and when they leave, you look forward to the next time they breeze back into your life.

More common, unfortunately, are people who we could describe as wet blankets and naysayers, effectively quashing joy, enthusiasm, and just about any other good thing you can think of whenever they show up. And sadly, there is no shortage of this kind of person in the church, in the pew, and even in lay leadership positions. These individuals criticize the sermon, complain about the music, question every decision that is made, and in general are anything but refreshing to be around. And with no lack of these people in the church, it is no wonder so many pastors leave the ministry.

A great—and simple—way to be a breath of fresh air to your pastor is with your words. As John Piper challenges, "Go out of your way to say some gracious words of encouragement [to him]. Write him a note [or e-mail]; call him up on the phone. Get him alone sometime, look him right in the face, and say, 'I appreciate your work, pastor, and I am praying for you every day.'"[39] Timely and intentional words of support remind the pastor that he is not alone, even in difficult times.

Onesiphorus is also a great example of the impact that the layperson can have in a pastor's ministry. He ministered to Paul by being loyal to and supportive of him, even when times got tough (he "was not ashamed of my chains" [2 Tim. 1:16 NIV]) and by going out of his way to meet Paul's needs ("sought me out very zealously and found me" [2 Tim. 1:17]). When his ministry was flourishing, Paul had plenty of people surrounding him. However, when things got tough, sadly, many abandoned the aging apostle. But not Onesiphorus; he remained supportive, refusing to be ashamed of his pastor, in spite of the fact that he was in prison, chained to a Roman soldier 24/7. Blessed is the pastor who has someone whom they can count on to support him, even (and especially) when times are tough.

Equally blessed is the pastor who has someone who makes meeting the pastor's needs a priority, even if it involves personal sacrifice. For some reason, upon arriving in Rome, Onesiphorus experienced great difficulty finding his former pastor, but he did not let that deter him. Rather, he "sought [Paul] out very zealously [until he] found [him]" (2 Tim. 1:17). I fear that few in our culture, which values convenience, personal creature comforts, and self-interest, would be zealous about anything that involved sacrifice and did not result in some level of self-gratification or satisfaction. If we are serious about ministering to those in pastoral ministry, we will have to "esteem others [i.e., our pastors] better than [ourselves and] look out not only for [our] own interests, but also for the interests of [our pastors]" (Phil. 2:3–4).

No doubt, pastors have a tough job: ministering to others can be demanding, exhausting, and sometimes thankless. Add to this the fact that pastors are frail human beings (Ps. 103:14–15), like the people they are called to serve, and it becomes clear that they need someone to minister to their specific needs just as much as we do. And the truth is, if you do not do it, you can be fairly certain no one else will.

Here are ten ways to minister to your pastor and church staff:

1. Pray for your pastor, his staff, and their families daily.

2. Give your pastor and staff the benefit of the doubt.

3. Be a discreet and trusted friend.

4. Volunteer to assist him and/or his family without waiting for an invitation.

5. Be a positive buffer between the pastor, staff, and the church body by heading off any attacks whenever possible.

6. Buy into the vision of the pastor and staff, even if you do not fully understand.

7. Give the pastor and staff the same respect that you desire, especially as it relates to solving disagreements.

8. Regularly provide expressions of encouragement (gifts, kind notes, etc.).

9. Before expressing your preferences, discern

between biblical "commands" and your own "opinion."

10. Most of all, always make sure that your pastor or staff member is given the authority needed to fulfill the responsibility that is thrust upon them.

Prison Ministry
Steve Cahill

[1] The Spirit of the Lord GOD is upon Me,
Because the LORD has anointed Me
To preach good tidings to the poor;
He has sent Me to heal the brokenhearted,
To proclaim liberty to the captives,
And the opening of the prison to those who are
    bound;
[2] To proclaim the acceptable year of the LORD,
And the day of vengeance of our God;
To comfort all who mourn,
[3] To console those who mourn in Zion,
To give them beauty for ashes,
The oil of joy for mourning,
The garment of praise for the spirit of heaviness;
That they may be called trees of righteousness,
The planting of the LORD, that He may be glorified.
—Isaiah 61:1–3

Overview

Prison/jail ministry is an oft-neglected ministry in the church. Most laypersons and pastors are uncomfortable in this setting. Perceived or actual red tape tends to discourage visitation. There is a stigma attached to incarceration and prison ministry. Avoiding this ministry is typical. Sometimes ministry to a prisoner feels like siding with the lawbreaker or against the crime victim. These emotional barriers build more walls of isolation for the incarcerated. Yet we are called to visit brothers and sisters who are in prison:

> [39] "'When did we see You sick, or in prison, and come to You?' [40] And the King will answer and say to them, 'Assuredly, I say to you, inasmuch as you did it to one of the least of these My brethren, you did it to Me.'" (Matt. 25:39–40)

The Holy Spirit beckons us to reach out to the lost in our penal institutions:

> [18] Now all things are of God, who has reconciled us to Himself through Jesus Christ, and has given us the ministry of reconciliation, [19] that is, that God was in Christ reconciling the world to Himself, not imputing their trespasses to them, and has committed to us the word of reconciliation.
> [20] Now then, we are ambassadors for Christ, as though God were pleading through us: we implore you on Christ's behalf, be reconciled to God. (2 Cor. 5:18–20)

If God has not counted our trespasses against us we ought not count prisoners' trespasses against them. These are hurting people who need to be reconciled to Jesus, church, society, family, and friends.

According to the Bureau of Justice Statistics, in 2008, 7.3 million Americans were under correctional supervision.[40] That means that one of every thirty-one adult Americans was under judicial supervision. These statistics continue to increase. This is a problem that is not going away soon. Every church and every community is affected.

These are ways we can answer God's call to minister to the incarcerated:

1. Pray for the incarcerated and their families.

2. Write letters of spiritual encouragement to inmates (I suggest men to men, women to women).

3. Encourage the inmate's family members. Witness to the unsaved and invite the unchurched to church.

4. Visit the incarcerated (I suggest men to men and women to women).

5. Represent Christ and the church to the incarcerated and their families (1 Cor. 5:12–13:12).

6. Model personal responsibility (1 Tim. 4:12).

7. Model forgiveness and acceptance (1 John 1:9).

8. Be a friend (Prov. 17:17).

9. Be a good listener (James 1:19).

10. Know your own weakness as you seek to help the inmate (Gal. 6:1).

Ministry Strategy

Initial Contact

I suggest initial contact to be through the mail. If you do not have an address or do not know where the inmate is located, most departments of correction and county jails have Web sites where you can get information. You will need the inmate's ID number and address; most facilities will not deliver mail if the inmate's ID number is not on the envelope. Before writing the letter pray for the inmate, and pray for wisdom. There are a few things you should and shouldn't do when writing a letter:

1. Do show concern for the inmate's spiritual well-being.

2. Do ask the inmate how you can pray for him or her and for specific prayer concerns.

3. Do inquire about the inmate's family.

4. Do inquire about institutional activities such as educational opportunities, recreation, chapel activities, and other rehabilitation programs.

5. Do share spiritual insights, scriptural helps, and personal testimonies, but do not be preachy.

6. Do not participate in anti-institution, anti-court, or anti-system sentiment.

7. Do not send money (it changes the dynamic of the relationship).

8. Do not agree to be a mediator between the inmate and his or her family or friends. He or she needs to take personal responsibility. Also, you do not want to pressure family or friends.

9. Do not allow the inmate to guilt you into anything. Some inmates will manipulate you and try to involve you in his or her schemes.

The Prison/Jail Visit

When you have decided to visit the inmate, go back to the prison's Web site and study the rules. In most prisons you have to fill out a visitor application form and mail it to the inmate's case manager. You must be approved to visit. The Web site will likely give you directions to the institution and explain to you how to make a reservation. Visits can last from one to six hours (you do not have to stay the whole time). Review the dos and don'ts for writing letters (they still apply).

There are a few things you should and shouldn't do when visiting an inmate:

1. Do pray with the inmate upon arrival and departure.

2. Do take a photo ID.

3. Do dress appropriately. Check the rules. Let modesty be your guide. You will likely have to

clear a metal detector. Do not wear steel-toe boots. Minimize jewelry.

4. Do leave all pocketknives, tools, and weapons at home.

5. Do not take anything into the facility except allowable items. Check the rules. Even Bibles and literature are not allowed in most facilities. Check with staff to see if a Bible is allowed or available in the visiting area.

6. Do take some change or a few dollars for refreshments. The inmate cannot purchase refreshments but you can usually offer him or her a refreshment.

7. Do not give the inmate anything, and do not take anything from him or her.

Closing Remarks

Remember your primary role is as a spiritual encourager and representative of Jesus and the church. Encourage the inmate to become responsible for himself or herself. Be an advocate for Christ. Avoid being the inmate's advocate to the institution, as it will change your role with the inmate. If you have questions concerning the inmate's spiritual needs, contact the prison chaplain. The chaplain is in charge of religious programming and policy.

Sometimes when church members visit inmates they sense a call to prison ministry. If you have this urge to get involved, contact the chaplain of the institution. There are several avenues for involvement such as one on one mentoring, group Bible studies, worship services, and seminars for inmates. Most chaplains are open to innovative and dynamic ministries.

Scripture

Salvation, "Romans Road": Romans 3:23; 5:8; 6:23; 10:9–10.

Forgiveness: Hebrews 10:17–18; James 5:20; 1 John 1:7–9; 2:1–2; Revelation 1:5.

Spiritual Strongholds: 2 Corinthians 10:3–5; Ephesians 6:10–18; 1 Thessalonians 5:8; Hebrews 4:12; 1 Peter 2:11.

Intercessory Prayer: John 17:9–26; Ephesians 3:11–12; 6:18–19; Philippians 4:6; 1 Timothy 2:1–3; Hebrews 4:16; James 5:14–16.

Same-Sex Attraction
Elton L. Moose

[26] Then God said, "Let Us make man in Our image, according to Our likeness; let them have dominion over the fish of the sea, over the birds of the air, and over the cattle, over all the earth and over every creeping thing that creeps on the earth." [27] So God created man in His own image; in the image of God He created him; male and female He created them.

—Genesis 1:26–27

Overview

Editor's Note: This focus of this chapter is not about developing a position about homosexuality. Rather, the focus is on ministering to those who have adopted the lifestyle and those who desire to come out of the lifestyle, and the family members of the person who has adopted this lifestyle.

Same-sex attraction, commonly called homosexuality, is the subject of much discussion, particularly in the past thirty years. After many years of silence, with the entrance of HIV/AIDS, the subject came to the forefront of discussions related to sexuality, society, and the church.

People on both sides of the issue have strong opinions and engage in fervent arguments. The subject of homosexuality divides every part of society. It reaches all the way from the government into the church. It divides families and friends. There are those who say people are born either gay or straight. There are others who believe it is caused by social and psychological influences. Research into homosexuality has not helped calm the heated debate between the opposing groups. No matter what side anyone takes, the issue of homosexuality must be dealt with in the family, church, and society as a whole.

Everyone will deal eventually with this subject in his or her lifetime. A child might come out to parents declaring he or she is gay. That family must learn how to handle their emotions and responses to an announcement that the son or daughter is gay. People in the workplace must learn how to deal with employees or employers who admit they are gay.

This article does not try to prove one side right or wrong. Instead the focus is on the importance of understanding different viewpoints in this debate and learning good responses.

Those who believe they are born homosexual desire acceptance. Many gay men and women say they have felt attracted to individuals of the same gender as long as they can remember. Gay men say they have always felt different from other boys. This is also true for gay women. Homosexuals desire equal treatment with others in society. Their stance is that they are a minority in society with rights that should be protected. In recent years homosexuals, their families, and friends have become more vocal in expressing this view.

Those who believe homosexuality is a social and psychological problem believe that certain dynamics within the family and community influence a person's perception of self and sexuality. Some of the causes discussed are that family dynamics create confusion about gender identity. A child who is neglected, physically abused, and/or shown partiality, among other things, may reject his or her own gender. A child who feels different from his peers may believe there is something wrong with himself or herself.

Many religious faiths believe that sexual activity outside of marriage, especially with someone of the same sex, is sinful. This has caused debate in many religious communities. People have strong feelings on both sides of this issue. Those who believe that homosexuality is social/psychological base their belief upon six stages to homosexual development:

1. Low self-esteem, which stems from a dysfunctional family environment.

2. Gender emptiness, in which the child feels rejected by those of the same gender.

3. Gender attraction, in which a person feels insecure with his or her own gender, leaving him or her to look to someone of the same gender to feel secure in himself or herself.

4. Sexual attraction, which occurs in adolescence, when the hormones begin to flow and sexual desires arise. Sex is confused with

intimacy and therefore in order to become intimate, it is believed that one must engage in sexual behavior. Often those attractions are toward those of the same sex.

5. Homosexual reinforcement, during which one engages in homosexual activity wherein the person begins to habituate and form a homosexual orientation.

6. Homosexual identity, which occurs when peace is achieved once a person gives in to his or her feelings and self-identify as being gay.

This information will assist families to understand the process through which their loved one moved to declare himself or herself gay.

Ministry Strategy

Family Response

The major reactions that parents experience are disbelief and questioning what they might have done wrong to cause their child to declare that he or she is gay. Some men respond in deep-seated anger, because they perceive the admission as a threat to their own sexuality. Parents need to find someone to talk with about their feelings. Pastors are good resources, but also Christian counselors. Because people often equate acceptance with condoning the behavior, parents often struggle with learning the difference between acceptance and condoning. The greatest need for a person who struggles with same-sex attraction is to believe that others, especially family, accept him or her. Those who have same-sex attraction can discern when parents and/or other family members treat them differently, and this difference can drive them away from the family. Parents of the same sex—fathers toward their sons or mothers toward their daughters should try to engage children in common activities. This must not be done in a pushy way or the child will resent the attention. If parents abused a child in the past, the first step in healing is to ask the child for forgiveness. Friends sometimes pull away from a person who says he or she is gay. Friends must realize that gayness is not contagious and that feelings of attraction toward someone of the same sex are internal; they cannot wipe off on others.

Another issue the parents will deal with is guilt. They wonder what they did wrong. A common response is to go on a mission to find "the solution." They want to find the fix.

Be aware of these things as you deal with the family members.

A Christian Response

Christians should manifest love toward anyone no matter what their belief about the subject. Accepting someone who is gay is not the same as condoning his or her lifestyle. The only way we can influence people for Christ is to show them love. When we demonstrate love, we gain the freedom to speak the truth in love. The first goal is to lead a person into a saving knowledge of Jesus

Christ as Lord and Savior. Christ within is the only possible way to change.

Not everyone who struggles with same-sex attraction wishes to live out their desires. Many of those who desire change do so for religious reasons; others want to change because they want to marry and have a family. Still others have experienced a lot of emotional strain within the lifestyle and wish to change their orientation. Below are some things you can do to help those who wish to come out of the lifestyle or who struggle with the desire but do not want to live it out:

1. Share the hope, power, and love found in Jesus Christ.

2. Encourage them to break all contact with homosexual companions who would tempt the individual to homosexual behavior. They need to also avoid all Web sites or material that promote homosexual behavior.

3. Get them to someone who can help them. There are organizations that will assist someone who wishes to be set free from the power of homosexuality in their lives. There is a group for almost every faith— Exodus International, Courage, Evergreen International, and Jonah. Scientific information and referrals can be obtained from the National Association for the Reparative Therapy of Homosexuality (NARTH). There

are also groups in most cities that offer support to those who wish to remain in a gay identity. Your church staff is also a valuable resource.

4. Be a friend and an encourager. The road is long, difficult, and lonely for the individual coming out of the lifestyle.

5. Help the person make right choices (Deut. 30:19).

6. Pray for and with the person. This is a spiritual battle (2 Cor. 10:3–5; Eph. 6:10).

There are things to avoid doing or saying:

1. Avoid condemning, as that is not helpful to the person. You can hold your position on the subject without condemning.

2. Do not say "a Christian shouldn't have those kinds of feelings." The truth is that many Christians do.

3. Do not make light or joke about homosexuality.

4. Do not tell the person all he or she needs to do is stop what he or she is doing or feeling. They do need to stop, but there are many complicated issues that lead a person to be attracted to someone of his or her own gender. Chances are the person probably has tried to quit because of fear of social ostracism,

but that attempt to change behavior can be unsuccessful.

The same principle applies to those who desire to change as toward those who do not want to change: love them.

Everyone has a deep need to be loved and accepted by family and friends. There are five human needs that apply to every person: survival, safety, love/belonging, good self-esteem, and self-actualization. If any of these needs are not met adequately, it causes people to react both emotionally and behaviorally. Too often, adults and children will act out inappropriately in order to meet a legitimate need. Everyone needs unconditional love. They need to have the ability to be able to trust others. People will respond better when they have the loyalty of family and friends. Everyone needs to have a place where they can be themselves and feel respected by others.

Scripture

Many of Jesus' teachings illustrate how we should treat others. The Beatitudes in Matthew 5, 6, and 7 are good examples to create a good attitude toward other people. One Scripture in particular is in Matthew 7:12, "Whatever you want men to do to you, do also to them, for this is the Law and the Prophets."

There are many Scriptures that speak about many forms of sexual immorality, including homosexuality: Romans 13:13; 1 Corinthians 6:9, 13, 18; 2 Corinthians 12:21; Galatians 5:19; Ephesians 5:3; Colossians 3:5;

1 Thessalonians 4:3; Hebrews 12:16; 13:4; and Revelation 21:8.

The Scriptures speak to the homosexual issue in both the Old and New Testaments: Genesis 19:4–13; Leviticus 18:22; 20:13; Romans 1:18–32; 1 Corinthians 6:9; and 1 Timothy 1:10.

It is clear in the Bible that God's intent from the beginning was for marriage to be between men and women. This truth was affirmed many times in the New Testament and by Jesus himself.

Additional Scriptures

For the person coming out of same-sex lifestyle:

Renewed Mind: Isaiah 26:3; Romans 12:1–2; Ephesians 4:22–24; 2 Corinthians 10:5

Loneliness: Isaiah 57:15; Jeremiah 23:23–24; Hebrews 13:5

Hope: Psalm 39:7; Romans 15:13; 1 Corinthians 6:11

For loved ones and friends:

Love: Mark 12:31; Romans 13:10
Forgiveness: Ephesians 4:32
Guilt/Condemnation: Romans 8:1

The major approach to either side of this issue is love. "Love your neighbor as yourself" (Matt. 22:39).

Sexual Addiction
Mark R. Laaser

[13] Has then what is good become death to me? Certainly not! But sin, that it might appear sin, was producing death in me through what is good, so that sin through the commandment might become exceedingly sinful. [14] For we know that the law is spiritual, but I am carnal, sold under sin. [15] For what I am doing, I do not understand. For what I will to do, that I do not practice; but what I hate, that I do. [16] If, then, I do what I will not to do, I agree with the law that it is good. [17] But now, it is no longer I who do it, but sin that dwells in me. [18] For I know that in me (that is, in my flesh) nothing good dwells; for to will is present with me, but how to perform what is good I do not find. [19] For the good that I will to do, I do not do; but the evil I will not to do, that I practice. [20] Now if I do what I will not to do, it is no longer I who do it, but sin that dwells in me.

[21] I find then a law, that evil is present with me, the one who wills to do good. [22] For I delight in the law of God according to the inward man. [23] But I see another law in my members, warring against the law of my mind, and bringing me into captivity to the law of sin which is in my members. [24] O wretched man that I am! Who will deliver me from this body of death? [25] I thank God—through Jesus Christ our Lord!

So then, with the mind I myself serve the law of God, but with the flesh the law of sin.

—Romans 7:13–25

Overview

It might seem strange on the surface to imagine that sex could become an addiction, but sex can become addictive when used to excess and when used as a way to escape pain and boredom in a similar way to how food, alcohol, and drugs can become addictive. While sex has been a problem since Adam and Eve became ashamed of their nakedness after the Fall, the Internet has rapidly accelerated the numbers of people caught in addiction.

There is hope because treatment for sex addiction has advanced in the last twenty-five years. I was fortunate to receive treatment for my own addiction and have now been free of my addiction for twenty-three years. Since that time God has allowed me to work in this field and with some of the most successful treatment leaders of our time.

What Is Sex Addiction?

Historically, the word *addiction* has been controversial in the Christian community. Some people fear the concept of addiction takes away personal responsibility for sinful behavior. They are concerned that people who call themselves addicts blame their personal decisions on an addiction. But all addicts who are truly repentant and want to change will accept personal responsibility for their actions. Keep in mind that there is a spectrum of addiction. People lose more and more of their ability to channel and redirect their sexual energy as the addiction progresses.

The medical and counseling community has established several universal criteria for determining if a substance or behavior is an addiction.

Use of the substance or behavior is an addiction when it has become unmanageable. This means that the addict has tried to stop, over and over again, but cannot. There is a history of failed attempts. The word *powerlessness* has also been used to describe this pattern. Sometimes addicts refer to themselves as "out of control." Christian sex addicts repeatedly try prayer, devotion, Bible study, and renewal of salvation without success.

Use of the substance or behavior is an addiction when the use gets worse over time. This means that more of the substance or behavior will be needed over time to achieve the same effect. The chemistry of the brain adjusts to whatever an addict puts into it. Over time the brain demands more to achieve the same effect. Thinking about sex and engaging in sexual behavior requires that the brain produce the brain chemistry to achieve sexual response. New research is finding that the sexual chemistry of the brain can also become tolerant, which means more and more stimulation is necessary to have the same brain chemistry effects: the feelings of arousal, excitement, and pleasure. This escalation can take two forms.

The most basic is that the addict does more of the same kind of behavior. An addict might start out masturbating once a month and progress to once or more a day in the course of his or her addiction.

For other addicts progression means that they will need new kinds of experiences to achieve the same high. So they will look for new, novel, or more risky forms of sexually acting out. Most every addict can point to certain behaviors that they at one time said they would never do, and later find themselves doing. It is important to note that, while this pattern of escalation helps explain how some addicts degenerate into offending behaviors, it is rare for this to happen. Only a very small percentage of sex addicts become sex offenders.

Because of the brain chemistry involved, addicts use the thoughts and behaviors that produce the neurochemical highs to either raise or lower their moods. This is what is meant by saying that addicts "medicate" their feelings. If an addict is depressed, lonely, or bored, he or she can think of exciting sexual encounters, either remembered or imagined, and the arousal part of the sexual response produces chemicals that raise his or her mood. If an addict is stressed, anxious, or fearful, he or she will tend to think of the relationship or romance quality of a sexual encounter. These associated brain chemicals create a feeling of well-being and contentment that lowers his or her mood. Most addicts are capable of both kinds of thoughts, and therefore can both raise and lower their moods depending on their feelings at the moment.

Finally, addicts act out despite negative consequences. Addicts do not pay attention to negative consequences and are in denial. They usually minimize or rationalize their acting out, despite the consequences. Until an addict decides to surrender control of the fears that prevent him or her from getting help, he or she will continue to act out. As the addict experiences more negative consequences for his or her behavior, feelings of depression and self-hatred will grow. Unless they are somehow helped to find hope and guidance for change, these negative feelings could create the fuel for further sexual acting out.

Ministry Strategy

In ministering to a sex addict it is most helpful to think of the addict, the addict's spouse, and the marriage of the addict and spouse. Some addicts come for help on their own. Some are discovered by their spouses. Extreme cases can require an intervention like with alcoholism.

Three Spiritual Questions

I believe that all sex addicts must answer three fundamental spiritual questions every day.

Do you want to get well? In John 5, Jesus asks a man who has been paralyzed for thirty-eight years if he wants to get well. A logical question might be why he would need to do so. Would not all paralyzed men want to be healed? Jesus knows that for some it is a question about motivation. A part of sex addicts want to be free of the problem as long as God does all the work. Otherwise, addicts may be what James calls "double-minded" (James 1:8). Some addicts are selfish enough to believe that their addiction is the way they

have controlled their emotions. They have not totally surrendered their lives, in this case their sexuality, to Christ.

What are you thirsty for? In John 4 Jesus tells a
woman, who has been married five times and who is
living with another man, that anyone who drinks of the
well by which they are standing will thirst again, but that
anyone who drinks of the "living water" of salvation will
never thirst. Addicts will need to ask themselves what
really satisfies their thirst for their needs: a relationship
with Christ or the next sexual encounter.

What are you willing to die for? In numerous places
in the Bible we are instructed to lead a life that imitates
Christ, thereby a willingness to die or be a sacrifice for
others. If addicts are to heal their selfishness, they must
ask themselves if they would die for others, including
their children and their spouses. The attitude of sacrifice
is necessary to make healthy choices.

Accountability

The book of Nehemiah contains the story of the
rebuilding of Jerusalem led by Nehemiah who had been a
servant in Persia.[41] The first six chapters that describe the
rebuilding of the wall around Jerusalem contain seven
principles for accountability. Accountability means that:

1. addicts must be broken, humble, and repentant;

2. addicts must be able to state their feelings and
   needs;

3. addicts will need a flock of support in the
   form of groups to help them. There are now

both twelve-step groups and Christ-centered support groups for sex addiction;

4. addicts will need to remove all the garbage from their lives. Their rituals or behaviors that lead to sexual sin will also need to be eliminated;

5. addicts need to plan ahead for times of attack or temptation. Waiting until those times come to make phone calls or ask for support is often too late;

6. addicts need to be encouraged to defend against temptation and to build positive and godly behaviors into their lives;

7. addicts must do whatever it takes to stay sober for as long as it takes. The work of healing may take the rest of a life and sometimes be expensive, but the work must continue.

Taking Every Thought Captive

Paul tells us in 2 Corinthians 10:5 that we must make all of our thoughts obedient to Christ. My belief is that usually we are told to simply stop our sexually sinful thinking by telling it go away. There are many spiritual disciplines like prayer and Bible study that can help make our thoughts obedient to Christ. I also believe, however, that it is very important to question the motivation of our thoughts. We will always find that even the most perverse thoughts represent a hunger in our souls for love, affirmation, and nurturing. If we can find healthy ways to receive those things from God and others, my experience is that the sinful thoughts will go away.

Often our sinful thoughts and fantasies are the result of the pain we have experienced in our early lives. They may be the result of those mistaken beliefs that we carry about ourselves. Healing these memories, what Alcoholics Anonymous calls "stinking thinking" is an essential part of the journey. I find that helping addicts experience the truth of God's love is essential. It is often helpful to ask an addict, "Despite what you believe about yourself, what message would Jesus like you to know?"

A Spouse's Needs

The spouse of someone who suffers from sexual addiction needs care as well.

The spouse has a need to have his or her pain heard. A spouse also needs the support of other people of his or her same gender who are dealing with the same situation. The addict must be totally broken and humble and to stay sober.

The spouse needs a complete disclosure of all the addict's sexual sins. This is a very controversial point but I believe that without disclosure, true intimacy and honesty will not happen. The spouse needs someone farther down the road of healing to hold the hope for him or her that the marriage can be restored.

The Three-Legged Stool

For the marriage of an addict and spouse to be saved, there must be three pieces in place just like the three legs of a stool. There must be the healing work that the addict does, the healing work that the spouse does, and the healing work that is done by the couple. Without equal amounts of energy being applied to each of these "legs," the marriage will not be saved. The couple should have at least one other couple to talk to who has survived this healing journey.

Scripture

Sexual Immorality: Matthew 5:32; 1 Corinthians 5:9–10; 6:13–20

Avoiding Adultery: Proverbs 5:3–8

Pure Thoughts: Philippians 4:8

Escaping Temptation: 1 Corinthians 10:30

Grace and Forgiveness: Romans 8:35–39

Imitating the Sacrifice of Christ: Ephesians 5:1–3

Resources

Books

Debbie Laaser, *Shattered Vows* (Grand Rapids: Zondervan, 2009).

Mark R. Laaser, *Healing the Wounds of Sexual Addiction* (Grand Rapids: Zondervan, 2005).

Mark R. Laaser and Debbie Laaser, *The Seven Desires of the Heart* (Grand Rapids: Zondervan, 2009).

Web sites

www.faithfulandtrueministries.com

www.freedomeveryday.org

Sexual Violence
Elton L. Moose

[3] For this is the will of God, your sanctification: that you should abstain from sexual immorality; [4] that each of you should know how to possess his own vessel in sanctification and honor, [5] not in passion of lust, like the Gentiles who do not know God; [6] that no one should take advantage of and defraud his brother in this matter, because the Lord is the avenger of all such, as we also forewarned you and testified. [7] For God did not call us to uncleanness, but in holiness.

—1 Thessalonians 4:3–7

Overview

Sexual violence is considered to be rape and/or sexual abuse. Rape and sexual abuse are both performed without the individual's consent. If alcohol or drugs are used to first dull a person's senses, it is still considered sexual violence since the person is unable to refuse the abuse in whichever form it takes.

Sexual violence causes the victim deep emotional pain and at times physical pain. The individual feels violated, used, betrayed, and shamed. Sexual violence diminishes a person's sense of self and is humiliating. Children who experience sexual violence often believe there is something wrong with them and that they deserved what was done to them. Sexual abuse in either boys or girls may cause them to question their sexual identity as they become confused about the abuse. Sometimes a child will reject his or her identity in order to protect himself or herself from the hurt from further sexual abuse. A child's sense of trust is violated, causing him or her not to trust adults, among other emotional responses. Often a child will pull away from any adult who resembles the perpetrator, or a child will act out in other irrational ways such as displaying angry outbursts without an apparent cause. Often children will begin failing in school because of the inner turmoil resulting from the abuse. The family and friends should be prepared for any unusual behavior. These outbursts also are a warning sign that the child has been abused in some form. Children who are sexually abused often do not tell any adults because of the fear of personal harm or harm to the child's family members. Many times, the perpetrator tells the child, "This is our secret." Sometimes the person will tell the child he or she will hurt a family member if the child tells. Perpetrators often believe that the individual wanted the abuse.

Many times, people will not report abuse because of the shame associated with abuse and this is especially true with rape. Children, especially, are reluctant to report abuse.

Rape and abuse are both against the law. Those who are raped or sexually abused should report such activity to the proper authorities. Adults who learn of child abuse should immediately call children's services and the police and report the abuse.

Ministry Strategy

Ministering to the Abused

If a child tells you she or he has been abused, the first response should be one of empathy and support toward the victim. Children tend to feel responsible for the abuse and they must be assured that they are not responsible. The child must be made to feel safe. The abuse must be reported to the appropriate people. If the abuse is reported to someone in the church, the child's parents should be contacted immediately and the church should support them as well. People's first response is usually one of unbelief, which is quickly followed by anger toward the perpetrator. This is a natural response.

Adults who have suffered abuse, whether physical, sexual, or both, feel a deep sense of shame. They feel violated. Sometimes, the emotional pain of abuse is so deep a person finds it extremely emotionally painful to talk about. Church leadership should utilize patience in such a case. Give the person space to talk or not to talk, but be there to support her or him.

Isaiah 51:3 is a helpful verse to use with the abused. Also recall that Jesus felt compassion toward those who were suffering. James 5:11 states that the Lord is compassionate and merciful. One concept that is used in helping victims is that Jesus wept as he viewed the abuse. The heart of a great God reaches out to those who have suffered abuse. Support and love anyone who is helping a victim of abuse. Never try to excuse the abuse, for the abused will feel she or he is not understood. Sometimes the abused wonders why God did not stop the abuse. Help that individual to realize that no one is on a puppet string and that even though the Lord is not pleased, He is there to give comfort and strength as she or he works though the abuse.

Another thing that can be done is to form a prayer support group for the abused. If the abused is a child, the support group may be for the parents. This all needs to be done discreetly and with the abused person's permission and input. Remember the abused probably does not want a lot of people to know what has happened.

Helping the Perpetrator

Sometimes you will find yourself dealing with the person who perpetrated the violence. The natural response is abhorrence or a sickening feeling. You probably will not want to have anything to do with the individual. If he or she has come to you and admitted committing sexual violence, whether it is rape or abuse, you must realize he or she is reaching out for help. You have the opportunity to help the person by leading him or her in the appropriate steps to take.

If the perpetrator is reporting that he or she abused or raped a child or raped an adult, it is your duty to advise him or her to turn himself or herself in to law enforcement. If he or she refuses to do it, you are required by law to report the abuse. Perpetrators should also be advised to engage in professional counseling in order to reduce the probability of re-offending.

Sexual sins have devastating consequences, but like any sin they are forgivable. Here is a process you can lead a person through. Lead the person through confession, repentance, forgiveness, sorrow, and restitution.[42]

1. Confession. God hears and forgives those who confess their sins to God (1 John 1:9; Prov. 28:13).

2. Repentance. This means accepting responsibility for any sexual sin (2 Cor. 7:10). Repentance is turning to God and turning away from the sin.

3. Forgiveness. People need to forgive themselves for involving others in their sin. Eventually, those who are victims of sexual sins must come to the place where they can forgive the perpetrator. Be patient with the victim at this point. Forgiveness releases her or him from the shame that accompanies sexual sins (Col. 3:13). Forgiving a perpetrator does not free the perpetrator from the consequences of his or her abuse. He or she still has to face God and the law for his or her wrongdoing.

4. Sorrow. Jesus promises healing to those who grieve the results of sexual sin (James 4:9–10).

5. Restitution. Those who engage in sexual sins should seek the Lord for help in how to perform restitution (Ezek. 33:14–16).

The process of forgiveness is in no way an attempt to minimize what the person has done or to allow him or her to escape the consequences. There are consequences but there is also forgiveness. Now more than ever is the time that the individual needs God.

The basis of human sexuality is illustrated in Genesis 1. God created the human family for relationships. God planned that a sexual relationship is to be experienced between a man and woman in the covenant of marriage. The sexual union is intended to help people express spiritual intimacy, emotional bonding, and personal fulfillment. Anything outside this is a sin against God and against another human being. Sexual immorality is spoken of in the New Testament many times. There are at least twenty passages that deal with sexual immorality. Paul, in 1 Corinthians 6:13 (NIV) states a central truth about sexual immorality: "the body is not meant for sexual immorality."

Emotional and spiritual healing are available through the grace of God to the victim of sexual violence and also to the perpetrator. The goal for each party is restoration. Restoration for the perpetrator does not leave him or her off the hook, because he or she still is responsible for personal behavior. There are consequences for a person's behavior even though he or she received God's forgiveness.

We should offer hope of emotional and spiritual healing to those who have been abused. We should offer hope of forgiveness to the perpetrator and encourage him or her to seek professional assistance. Spending time with anyone who is abused assists her or him through the trauma of the abuse.

A Scripture that is especially helpful to the abused is Romans 8:31–39. Abuse does not separate anyone from the love and care of God in Christ Jesus. A person who works with children will have to explain that God loves them and is not pleased with the abuse. Assure the children that God loves them and He is not rejecting them.

Scripture

Forgiveness: Matthew 6:12, 14, 15; Ephesians 4:31–32

Fear: Psalm 34:4, 5; Romans 8:15; 2 Timothy 1:7; Hebrews 13:5–6

Trust God: Psalm 118:8–9; Proverbs 3:5–6; Isaiah 26:4

Peace: Psalm 4:8; Isaiah 26:3–4; Galatians 5:22–23

God's Care/Comfort: Isaiah 66:13; Matthew 11:28; 2 Corinthians 1:3–4

Healing: Isaiah 53:5; Luke 4:18–19

Special Needs
David Wheeler

³ Then the king said, "Is there not still someone of the house of Saul, to whom I may show the kindness of God?" And Ziba said to the king, "There is still a son of Jonathan who is lame in his feet."

—2 Samuel 9:3

Overview

Individuals with special needs and their families represent one of the largest unchurched people groups in the United States. With this in mind, it is imperative that local congregations catch the vision and learn to minister to this group through the love and compassion of Christ. According to special education teachers and those fluent in this kind of ministry, the most effective approach is family-to-family (relational) contact through genuine concern and servant-oriented ministries.

A Dose of Reality

I recall walking through a Mexican restaurant one day in Fort Worth, Texas, when I passed a young girl sitting in a wheelchair. I proceeded to engage the girl and her family by asking if I could speak to the "most beautiful young lady in the restaurant." The girl smiled as I introduced myself to her and the parents by letting them know that I have a special-needs child, Kara, who has mild cerebral palsy.

I then proceeded to ask the family about their involvement in a local church. Knowing the horrible track record of many congregations over the years in relating and adapting to special-needs families, I was not surprised at the immediate and awkward silence. It was only after I gently pushed for a response that the parents finally replied with the statement, "We used to attend." Eventually, they shared with a note of confusion how their eight-year-old daughter could be lovingly mainstreamed into a public school (secular) classroom, but was ignored and forced to remain in the nursery at church.

As the parent of a special-needs child, you can imagine the horror and embarrassment I felt for Christ's body, the church, when I heard the above story. Unfortunately, based on statistics and personal experience, this is an all too common testimony of many families. Along the same lines, I recently met a beautiful sixteen-year-old girl with mild Down syndrome at a local church. Her parents were brokenhearted about the apparent indifference of the youth group. We watched with great disappointment as the young woman stood alone after lunch without the slightest attempt from the youth group (or anyone else for that matter) to engage her in conversation or to invite her to join their activities. To them, she might as well have been invisible.

Ministry Strategy

Initiating a Special-Needs Ministry

There are several steps to take to begin an effective special-needs ministry. To begin with, one must clear up any misconceptions relating to special-needs individuals. First, most people tend to lump all impairments into the same category with the assumption that physical needs are always related to mental deficiency. Nothing could be further from the truth. Like everyone else, special-needs children and adults must be dealt with individually. The truth is, those with physical or mental challenges need the saving grace of the gospel message. In many cases, these individuals will excel beyond their supposed difficulties and often become bold evangelists and compassionate ministers of the gospel.

This leads to the second misconception that somehow special-needs individuals must always have limitations placed upon their activities and behavior. This is a wrong assumption. If you are the Christian parent of a special-needs child, or a layperson in a local church with the privilege of mobilizing people into ministry, please know that, like all other Christians, those with physical or mental impairments must also be obedient to the call of God upon their lives. This means that the church must not limit their community involvement in ministry for the sake of protecting a person who has a special need. In most cases, these individuals can be very effective in ministry and often become an asset to the outreach and caring ministry of the church.

For instance, suppose there is a family dealing with a special-needs situation in your community. Who could be better prepared to minister to this family evangelistically? They already understand many of the difficulties and challenges. It only takes a sacrifice of time, a strong trust in God, genuine concern, and a willingness to listen and get involved in kingdom business. In the end, this will rebuild the family atmosphere of your church, create lasting memories, and develop a greater confidence among both the physically and mentally challenged, as well as the family members involved.

Consider the testimony of one family of a child with cerebral palsy who participated in door-to-door servant evangelism projects by allowing their excited young girl to be the first person met at the door bearing gifts. In one case it was fudge at Christmas, in another instance it was batteries for smoke detectors, or bags of microwave popcorn with a card attached stating "Pop in and visit our church some time." Those visited were introduced to each participant, given a special gift by a "special" child, and then told that "Christ loved them." In some of those cases they prayed with individuals; in others, they were able to share the gospel. In every instance, the participants learned the same important lessons about fulfilling the Great Commission, regardless of physical or mental limitations. Both the young girl and those visited received an extraordinary blessing. Imagine what would happen if the lay leaders of your church adopted these individuals and volunteered to go with the families as they ministered in the community.

A third misconception, and probably the most disheartening, is the idea that since one does not know what to say to a person with a special need, the best thing to do is to not say anything at all. Unfortunately, this approach often comes across as rude or indifferent. Worst of all, it usually results in staring, which magnifies the situation and makes the person with the special need feel even more self-conscience and out of place.

I recall one evening shortly after our four-year-old special-needs daughter learned to walk. We celebrated by going to her favorite restaurant. As she walked out of the restaurant, she insisted, as always, on "doing it herself." So we held the front doors open wide as she stumbled out, nearly falling several times. A young couple stood over to the side and rudely glared at Kara as we celebrated her independence. To say the least, I was irritated by the couple who stared and never smiled or offered a word of encouragement. It was then that I walked over to them and made the statement, "I am very sorry for the way Kara is walking. I told her to get away from the bar or this [stumbling] would be the result." The look on their faces was priceless.

In most cases, a proper response is to simply ask the person about her or his malady, or better yet, offer assistance if needed. Let the person tell her or his story while you be a good listener. Whatever you do, speak plainly (not slowly) and be yourself. People with special needs are like everyone else; they want to be loved and they need a relationship with Christ.

A Few Suggestions for Lay Ministries

As far as ministering within special-needs situations, consider several options like providing "parents' night out" opportunities, especially where the needs are chronic and demand round-the-clock care. I recently heard of a family like this where the parents had not been alone in more than three years because of required round-the-clock care. No wonder the divorce rate for parents of special-needs children is so high.

In some cases, the situation may demand securing a nurse who is trained to administer proper care. In many other situations you may only require a mild dose of patience, a listening ear, and a special ability to administer the love of Christ. Ask the Lord to show you how to proceed.

You might also consider preparing meals, mowing yards, offering to do small repair jobs, or providing some new clothes. If they are good quality, consider offering some of the slightly used clothes that your children have outgrown. In addition, one person expressed the need for volunteers to do grocery shopping. By the way, always be careful to respect handicap parking at the mall, church, or at the grocery store.

In addition, go through your church and ask for an honest assessment related to the accessibility needs of the disabled. Be open about negative attitudes and fears. Lead the way in educating your church. Contact Joni and Friends on the Internet (www.joniandfriends.org), or secure a local special-education teacher to lead the training. You can also provide free community education for parents of special-needs children about federal laws, public programs, and how to best represent their children.

Most important, do not give up even if the special-needs family does not respond immediately. Remember, above all people, they know the difference between loving concern and pity. These individuals do not need our pity. On the contrary, they need Jesus and the affirmation of dignity, love, compassion, and self-worth that is inherent to the gospel.

Final Suggestions

Ministering to the disabled is not complicated. Always remember there is no one-size-fits-all solution. You must plan to minister to the whole family, not just the person with the disability. Begin by researching community-based opportunities for ministries. Start by asking questions. Care. Be honest about your attitudes and prejudices. As a goal, seek to include and engage the disabled and their families into the ministries of the church. In doing so, you will help them find their ultimate fulfillment in Christ. Be proactive.

Scripture

Value of Life: Genesis 1:26–27; Psalm 139:13–14

God's Grace: Proverbs 3:34; 2 Corinthians 12:9–10; 2 Timothy 2:1; James 4:6

God's Plan: Jeremiah 29:11; Ephesians 2:10

God's Power: Psalm 68:35; 2 Corinthians 9:8

God Using One to His Glory: John 9:1–5

God Upholds: 2 Chronicles 16:9; Psalm 37:17; Isaiah 41:10

Ultimate Healing: Isaiah 35:5–10

Substance Abuse

James L. Smith

[20] And Noah began to be a farmer, and he planted a vineyard. [21] Then he drank of the wine and was drunk, and became uncovered in his tent.

—Genesis 9:20–21

Noah, a man of God, is the first person recorded in the Bible as being drunk from too much wine. The Bible has strong prohibitions against drunkenness. The apostle Paul admonished the believer not to get drunk on wine, but rather to be filled with the Holy Spirit (Eph. 5:18). The Christian is called to a godly, clear-headed life in order to be responsive to the promptings of the Holy Spirit.

Overview

Substance abuse affects millions of lives in the United States annually resulting in accidents, deaths, child abuse, spouse abuse, divorces, and loss of productivity, to name just a few of the problems. It profoundly influences individuals mentally, emotionally, physically, and spiritually.

Christians are not exempt from this issue regardless of the doctrinal views that they hold related the use of substances, particularly alcohol. Many believers have struggled with using alcohol and other drugs at some point in their lives. Some continue to struggle to maintain abstinence, while still others have relatives who are enslaved by addictions.

Substance abuse is a pattern of drug use that takes many forms ranging from taking more aspirin than the prescribed dose to injecting oneself with heroin.

Common substances that one abuses include alcohol, nicotine, caffeine, prescription medications, illicit drugs, over-the-counter (OTC) products, gasoline, and even household aerosol products. The common denominator is that each one changes the mood of the users. Moods can vary from feeling energetic, relaxed, peaceful, or euphoric to feeling lethargic, angry, fearful, agitated, paranoid, or depressed.

Symptoms

In general, any pattern of drinking or use of a substance (prescribed or illegal) that disrupts one's personal life and work is in question. If the substance abuser makes a variety of excuses pertaining to his or her behaviors, this should increase suspicions. Although lay ministers cannot diagnose, they can, in a caring way, point out the obvious.[43]

Watch for comments from peers of substance abusers like "He can sure handle his liquor," or "She drinks like a man." If the user's name appears in the local newspaper under "arrests," a visit from a lay minister may be in order.

Both substance abuse and dependence have dire consequences, among them, alienation from God, others, and self. These are the openings that the lay minister can address. How is it with their souls? This type of approach may lead to a discussion of problems related to substance abuse.

The numbers are staggering. The Substance Abuse and Mental Health Services Administration (SAMHSA) released the results of the *2008 National Survey on Drug Use and Health: National Findings*. In the United States, "an estimated 22.2 million persons (8.9 percent of the population aged 12 or older) were classified with substance dependence or abuse."[44] This means that for every 100 parishioners in a church, 9 have a serious problem.

Use of pain medications in a nonprescribed way is an example of substance abuse. This includes taking pain medications for the effect. Biting rather than swallowing a time-released medication like Oxycontin causes all the medication to be released at once creating a heroin-like rush. Many have died from strokes or heart failure from this practice.

Abuse includes the use of street drugs. Anyone who purchases from a dealer has no guarantee of the substance's quality, potency, or even its contents.

Inhaling or huffing substances around the home is another example of substance abuse. The inhalation of gasoline, household-cleaning products, compressed air used to dust off computer hardware, and even air conditioner refrigerant can cause irreversible brain damage in many, as well as death.

Common symptoms include:

- Changes in moods
- Muscle coordination problems
- Noticeable changes in reasoning
- Inappropriate or out-of-the-ordinary changes in behavior

The risk of substance abuse increases when an authority figure failed to teach values about the use of any substance. If a peer or someone in the home exposes a person to abuse the risk increases. Using substances to cope with mental health and physical conditions can lead to abuse as well.

Related Risks to Substance Abuse

Substance abuse is a high-risk behavior. When someone is in an altered state he or she has an increased chance of becoming a victim of crimes such as robbery or rape. There is an increased risk of suicide as a result of compromised reasoning and lowered inhibitions.

There is a greater chance of child abuse and spousal abuse. A substance abuser has a higher chance of participating in reckless behaviors, including sexual or illegal activities. There is always a risk of accidental overdose.

Can a Person Who Is Addicted Be Cured?

What do we mean by "cured"? There is no infection to treat or broken bone to set, but if a person stops using and maintains abstinence, he or she can recover.

Frequently, individuals in treatment will say that they are "recovering" rather than use terms like "recovered" or "healed." This frame of reference is very important to them because they understand that returning to occasional drug use or drinking socially is never an option. It is important for the lay minister to respect this frame of reference.

Treatment Options

Numerous treatment options are available:

- Intensive inpatient programs that provide structure, safety, and accountability
- Intensive Outpatient Programs (IOP) that meet several times per week, three to four hours each time, allowing the person to continue work and family responsibilities
- Individual counseling with an addiction specialist
- Support groups such as Alcoholics Anonymous (AA), Christian Recovery, and Christ-centered twelve-step programs
- Christian long-term care such as Teen Challenge that has programs for adults as well as teens

Ministry Strategy

As a lay minister you should educate yourself about addictions. Learn signs and symptoms. Attend support groups such as AA open meetings. Know available community resources. Display pamphlets in the church. Invite speakers for lay ministry training events. Add substance abuse resources to the church library.

Building relationships with all members will open doors to minister. As trust develops, you will discover that some have been ashamed to tell about substance abuse in the family or have wanted to protect a loved one's reputation in the church.

You are one who comes in the name of the Lord. Offer the hope that only the Lord can provide. Support the family members, both those who use and those who do not use substances. As the Holy Spirit directs, introduce them to Jesus Christ. Here is a list of things you should do:

- Establish rapport. Substance abusers must know that you care before you address any issues.
- Ask how you might help.
- It is crucial to remember that if the person wants help, assist her or him in contacting treatment resources immediately. This window of opportunity passes very quickly if you delay.
- If the substance abuser is dishonest, do not take this personally, and do not argue to convince him or her otherwise. This person lies more to self than to others in order to justify continued use.
- Recovering addicts are emotionally vulnerable. Lay ministers should work with persons of

the same sex. Paul admonishes us to avoid the appearance of evil (1 Thess. 5:22).

- Be prepared for a long-term commitment. Relapse can occur several times before the person becomes steadfast in sobriety. Be the friend who sticks closer than a brother (Prov. 19:24).
- You cannot "fix" the person. A temptation for Christian helpers is to believe that they could have prevented the person from relapsing.
- You are not a physician, mental health professional, or an attorney. Do not give advice in these areas. Refer to professionals for such issues. Provide a list of several professionals from which the person can choose. The person can make a choice rather than being told who to see.
- Substance abusers can easily manipulate others. Do not provide money or make excuses for their behaviors.
- Speak the truth in love (Eph. 4:15). Help abusers to understand the direct link between current problems and substance use.
- Pray regularly for those who begin to build drug-free lifestyles.
- Encourage abusers to make lifestyle changes that reduce the risk of temptation to relapse. For example, avoid sporting events with drinking buddies. Do not keep memorabilia that symbolizes partying, such as T-shirts with

beer logos or ornate pipes that were used for
marijuana.

- Celebrate significant periods of abstinence
  such as one day, one week, one month, three
  months, six months, or one year with words of
  encouragement, a phone call, a card, or a visit.
- When possible, provide care to the person's
  family members.

Within your church community you should recruit
members who have experience and compassion related
to substance abuse. Create an atmosphere of care in the
church by developing Christian support groups or by
making the building available to fellowships such as AA.
Provide activities as alternatives to partying for adults
as well as teens. Critical times would include after high
school athletic events and national holidays.

Jesus Christ died for the substance abuser. Tragically,
many will die from the use of chemicals, but there are
also those who will be thankful that lay ministers walked
alongside them as they found wholeness and freedom in
the Lord.

Scripture

Hope: Romans 5:8; 8:31; 2 Corinthians 5:17
Salvation: Luke 19:9–10
Healing: Matthew 4:23; James 5:16
Transformation: Romans 12:1–2; Philippians 4:8
Power: Acts 1:8; Ephesians 5:18

Temptation: 1 Corinthians 10:13; Hebrews 2:18; 4:15; James 4:7

Confrontation: John 5:6; 6:25–29

Drunkenness: Romans 13:13–14; 1 Peter 4:1–6

Resources

Substance Abuse and Mental Health Services Administration (SAMHSA): http://www.samhsa.gov

U.S. Department of Health and Human Services (HHS): http://www.hhs.gov

National Institute on Drug Abuse (NIDA): http://www.nida.nih.gov

Teen Challenge: http://teenchallengeusa.com

American Association of Christian Counselors: http://www.aacc.net

American Association of Pastoral Counselors: http://aapc.org

Alcoholics Anonymous: http://www.aa.org

Al-Anon, Alateen: http://www.al-anon.alateen.org

Suffering
Fred Milacci

[11] Now when Job's three friends heard of all this adversity that had come upon him, each one came from his own place—Eliphaz the Temanite, Bildad the Shuhite, and Zophar the Naamathite. For they had made an appointment together to come and mourn with him, and to comfort him. [12] And when they raised their eyes from afar, and did not recognize him, they lifted their voices and wept; and each one tore his robe and sprinkled dust on his head toward heaven. [13] So they sat down with him on the ground seven days and seven nights, and no one spoke a word to him, for they saw that his grief was very great.

—Job 2:11–13

Overview

Your phone rings. As soon as you answer, you immediately recognize the voice on the other end as that of your good friend, and he is obviously distraught. You do not catch all the details, but what is clear is that something awful has happened, and your friend is hurting deeply. Almost instantaneously, your mind is flooded with lots of questions including (but certainly not limited to) What should I say? What should I do? And perhaps most important, Why is he calling me and not a pastor or counselor?

Good questions, indeed—especially the last one. The truth is, however, helping those who are hurting is not something only pastors and counselors are called to do; it is a responsibility and privilege we all share. As Paul admonishes, all Christians are expected to "rejoice with those who rejoice, and weep with those who weep" (Rom. 12:15); it comes with being part of one body in Christ.

Also true is the fact that all of us—including and perhaps especially followers of Christ—will experience suffering regularly throughout our lifetimes; this is a direct result of being fallen people who live in a fallen world. Unfortunately, there are some Christians who seem to think that their position as children of God somehow exempts them from suffering. Nothing could be further from the truth; being a Christian does not exempt us from experiencing the hurts and pains of this world. Rather, as the apostle Peter warns, Christians should expect suffering to happen to them and even rejoice that they are able to identify with Christ in His sufferings (1 Peter 4:12–13).

In light of this, Drs. Tim Clinton and Ron Hawkins[45] suggest that Christians who desire to help those who are hurting should develop a "theology of suffering," a way of looking at and responding to this age-old problem in a way that is theologically correct, yet at the same time, immensely practical. They go on to state that a biblical perspective of suffering sees suffering as a privilege, part of following in Jesus' footsteps (1 Peter 2:21), an opportunity for both personal and spiritual growth (2 Cor. 12:9–10), an occasion to bring God glory (John 9:1–3), and/or a chance for the sufferer to be able to help others when they encounter pain and loss in their lives (2 Cor. 1:3–5).

It is that last point that I want us to focus on in the remaining part of this chapter. Put another way, if we are to fulfill our calling and responsibility as Christ followers, we need to find out how we can effectively minister to those who are suffering.

Ministry Strategy

If there was ever a person who experienced pain and suffering, it was the Old Testament character Job. Interestingly, even in Job's darkest hour, it was not a religious leader who came to comfort him; instead it was his three friends, Eliphaz, Bildad, and Zophar. There is good and bad to be learned from Job's three friends about helping those who are hurting. Here are three of the more salient lessons.

Be There

One of the greatest gifts we can give those who are hurting is simply our presence. Upon hearing of his troubles, Job's three friends immediately dropped whatever it was they were doing and left the comfort of their own homes to be with him when and where (location-wise) he was hurting. They did not wait for Job to reach out to them; rather, they took the initiative to go to him, just so they could be there with their friend in his time of grief and loss.

This is a lesson I learned early on in my adult life when a close friend of mine lost his forty-year-old wife to a massive heart attack. He called me, and I dropped what I was doing to meet him at the hospital where we walked for hours around the parking lot—him weeping uncontrollably and me praying frantically, having absolutely no idea what to do or say. After a while, however, it dawned on me that my friend did not need or want me to do or say anything; all he wanted was someone who would listen to him and provide a shoulder to lean on. It was a lesson that has served me well ever since: when people are suffering, often there is no substitute for a friend who is willing to just be there.

Be Quiet

Not only did Job's friends come to be with him in his hour of need, but according to Job 2:13, "they sat down with him on the ground seven days and seven nights, and no one spoke a word to him." Can you imagine that? The three of them sat there with their friend who was immersed in grief for seven days and seven nights, never saying anything. Many—if not most—of us cannot imagine doing that, probably because we jam-pack our lives with noise and other distractions. Not only that, but as a society, it seems as if we are uncomfortable with silence, even for a few minutes, let alone for an entire week. Then too, when people are hurting, for some reason we feel like we just have to say something, regardless of whether or not we have something of value to say.

Incidentally, if the story had ended here, with Job's three friends sitting in silence while he grieved, they probably would be remembered as some of the greatest friends in all of Scripture. It was not until they broke their silence and began to speak, attempting to explain why Job was suffering and to give him some unsolicited advice, that they got themselves in trouble—with both their friend and the Lord. If we are to effectively minister to the suffering, we would do well to learn from their mistake and instead follow James's wise counsel to be "swift to hear, [and] slow to speak" (James 1:19).

Be Encouraging

Without question, one of the best ways to minister to those who are hurting is by intentionally seeking tangible ways to be an encouragement to them in their time of need. In fact, as William Barclay notes:

> One of the highest of human duties is the duty of encouragement … it is easy to discourage others. The world is full of discouragers. [But] we have a Christian duty to encourage one another. Many a time a word of praise or thanks or appreciation or cheer has kept a man on his feet. Blessed is the man who speaks such a word.[46]

I realize that on the surface, this particular strategy may seem rather obvious. But quite frankly, sometimes we—yes, including and especially we Christians—can be more of a discouragement to those who are suffering than an encouragement, especially with our words.

That was certainly true of Eliphaz, Bildad, and Zophar. Originally, Job's three friends "made an appointment together to come and mourn with him, and to comfort him" (Job 2:11); in other words, they set out to encourage Job. And initially, by being empathetic (mourning with him and lifting their voices and weeping) and sympathetic (comforting him), no doubt they were an encouragement to him. But sadly, somewhere along the way, they forgot about encouraging and instead morphed into advising, criticizing, judging, and even condemning their friend; not exactly what a person who has just lost everyone he loves and everything he owns needs to hear. It is no surprise, then, that later Job refers to his friends as "miserable comforters" (Job 16:2*b*), admonishing that if the shoe were on the other foot and they were the ones who were suffering, he "would strengthen [i.e., encourage] [them] with [his] mouth, and the comfort of [his] lips would relieve [their] grief" (Job 16:5).

Those who are suffering do not need our advice (in spite of how badly we want to give it), our explanations for why they are suffering, our analysis of their situation, or even a sermon; in fact, they may not even need us to quote Scripture to them. Instead, as Chuck Swindoll advises, what people in pain need is our "compassion. A touch of kindness. A gentle, considerate, soft spoken word of assurance. Something to cushion the blows."[47] Or, as Solomon in his book of wisdom writes, "Ointment and perfume delight the heart, and the sweetness of a man's friend gives delight by hearty counsel" (Prov. 27:9).

Summary

Remember these five things when ministering to those who are suffering:

1. Ministering to the suffering is for all Christians, not just for pastors and counselors.

2. To effectively minister to the suffering, it is wise to think about and develop a theology of suffering.

3. One of the best things to do for those who are suffering is simply be there—with them and for them—in their time of pain.

4. When ministering to the suffering, it is better to do more listening and less talking.

5. Our primary goal in ministering to the suffering should be to provide comfort and encouragement, not our analysis, opinion, or advice.

Scripture

Prayer: Psalms 10:17; 22:24; 69:1; 102:1–28; James 5:13
Sympathy: 1 Corinthians 12:26
Christ's Aid: Hebrews 2:17–18; 4:14–16
Christ's Suffering: Isaiah 53:3–5; Hebrews 2:10
God's Comfort: 2 Corinthians 1:3–7

God's Grace: 1 Peter 5:10

God's Power: 2 Corinthians 4:7–12

God's Deliverance: Psalms 34:19; 116:1–19

God Sees: Psalm 31:7

God's Work of Refinement: Isaiah 48:10; Romans 5:3–5; 1 Peter 1:6–7

Nothing Is Comparable to Heaven's Glory: Romans 8:18; 2 Corinthians 4:16–18; 1 Peter 4:13

Nothing Can Separate Us from Christ: Romans 8:35–39

Patience: Romans 12:12

Suicide
Kent Spann

[3] The battle became fierce against Saul. The archers hit him, and he was severely wounded by the archers. [4] Then Saul said to his armorbearer, "Draw your sword, and thrust me through with it, lest these uncircumcised men come and thrust me through and abuse me." But his armorbearer would not, for he was greatly afraid. Therefore Saul took a sword and fell on it. [5] And when his armorbearer saw that Saul was dead, he also fell on his sword, and died with him.

—1 Samuel 31:3–5

Overview

There is nothing as earth-shattering as getting a call from a friend or acquaintance late one night who says, "It is not worth it anymore. I am going to take my life tonight." What do you do when that call comes? What do you do when you receive the call that someone in your church has committed suicide? There is nothing as stressful as dealing with someone who is suicidal.

More than 30,000 people commit suicide annually in the United States. It is estimated that a person dies by suicide every eighteen minutes. An attempt to commit suicide is made once every minute. According to the Centers for Disease Control and Prevention, it was the eleventh leading cause of death for all ages in 2006.[48] It is the third-leading cause of death for fifteen- to twenty-four-year-olds, and the sixth-leading cause of death for five- to fourteen-year-olds according to the American Academy of Child and Adolescent Psychiatry.[49] Those numbers reflect the number of people who actually commit suicide. More than 395,000 people are treated with self-inflicted injuries in emergency rooms each year.

These suicides are found in Scripture: Samson (Judg. 16:23–30), Saul (1 Sam. 31:4), Saul's armorbearer (1 Sam. 31:5), Ahithophel (2 Sam 17:23), Zimri (1 Kings 16:18), and Judas Iscariot (Matt. 27:5).

What Is Suicide?

The obvious answer to that question is the deliberate taking of one's own life. But it is more than that. To the person contemplating suicide it is the answer. It is the only answer to the person who sees no answer in this life to the problems, issues, suffering, or dilemmas he or she faces. Friedrich Nietzsche, the famous nineteenth-century German philosopher, said, "The thought of suicide is a great consolation: by means of it one gets successfully through many a bad night."[50] He is also the man who made famous the statement "God is dead."[51]

Suicide is an escape route. It is an answer. It is relief. It is the height of self-centeredness. It is the conclusion that life is not turning out the way the person wanted. It is a way out of the pain and suffering that comes with life on this fallen planet (Job 5:7).

Reasons People Attempt Suicide

It is hard for those who have never contemplated suicide to understand what is going on in the life of a person who attempts or commits suicide. There are many reasons but here are just a few:

- depression
- guilt
- loneliness such as after the death of a longtime spouse
- abuse, either sexual, emotional, or mental
- despair and hopelessness
- overwhelming circumstances such as the loss of a job, a financial collapse, and so forth
- grief
- mental disorders
- substance abuse
- failures in life such as a moral failure or a business failure
- suffering

While none of these is sufficient reason for one to take his or her life, it is important for the one helping the suicidal person to be understanding of what may be going on in this person's life.

Suicide and the Bible

It is important for the Christian leader who cares for the suicidal person to have a biblical perspective on suicide that is really more of a perspective on life. The biblical perspective on life is that it is sacred because people are made in the image of God. Therefore the taking of life, whether by murder or suicide, is prohibited (Gen. 1:27; 5:1; 9:6).

"Is suicide the unpardonable sin?" This question is frequently asked, especially by the survivors of suicide. They are referring to the passage in Matthew 12:31–32. The answer to the question is no. The Scriptures do not say it is the unpardonable sin. It is a sin, but it is not the unpardonable sin.

Myths About Suicide

There are many myths and misconceptions when it comes to suicide. You must be aware of these as you deal with the suicidal.

1. People who talk about committing suicide do not actually do it. The misconception is that people talk about suicide to get attention. While that may be the case sometimes, the reality is that those who talk about it do carry through on what they say.

2. People who are suicidal are certain to commit suicide. The truth is most do not really want to commit suicide or die; they just want hope or relief.

3. Certain types of people commit suicide. This implies that certain types of people are

immune to it. No one is immune. All types of people commit suicide.

4. Suicide is an impulsive act. The reality is that most suicides occur after long periods of planning or consideration.

5. Talking to someone about suicide may give the person the idea to commit suicide. This is simply not true. Oftentimes, talking about it gives the suicidal person relief from the anxiety.

6. A failed suicide attempt means the person was not really trying. While he or she did not succeed, the attempt was made.

Ministry Strategy

There are three different aspects of suicide in which you may be called upon to minister.

Before a Suicide

You may be called on before suicide has been committed. Here you are dealing with the person who is contemplating or even attempting to commit suicide. If you must care for a suicidal person, this is the point at which you want to deal with him or her.

The first thing you have to do when dealing with a suicidal person is to assess the situation. Assessment answers two questions: "Is the person at risk of committing suicide?" and "How serious is he or she?" There are some questions that will help you assess the situation.

1. Has the person already acted to commit suicide such as by taking pills or loading a weapon?

2. Has the person attempted suicide before?

3. Has anything traumatic happened recently in the life of the person such as death, the break up of a relationship, job loss, and so forth?

4. Have you or someone close to the person observed a marked change of personality or behavior in him or her?

5. How long has the person been thinking about suicide?

6. Is he or she intoxicated or on drugs?

7. Does the person have any mental condition that you are aware of? For example, is the person bipolar, depressed, or so forth?

The purpose of your assessment is not to make a psychological diagnosis. Leave that to the professionals. The purpose of your assessment is to know how to proceed in the immediate situation.

After assessing the situation your main role is to intervene so the threat of suicide is not carried out.

1. Take any suicidal talk or behavior seriously.

2. If the person has already acted to commit suicide (taken pills, cut himself or herself, etc.), you should find out where the person is

and call emergency services immediately. If you are on the phone with the person, have someone call emergency services for you.

3. Stay with him or her whether on the phone or in person.

4. Listen patiently. When dealing with a suicidal person, you have to be a good listener. If the person has contacted you, he or she is looking for someone to listen. Do not minimize the person's feelings. Let him or her get the anger or hurt out. Chances are if he or she continues to talk, the person will not commit suicide.

5. Assure the person that there is hope. Suicidal people need hope. Their world is full of despair at that moment (Jer. 20:14–18; Job 3:11–13). The Christian message is a message of hope (see the Scriptures). Let him or her know God really does love and care even though this may not seem evident to the person at the time.

6. Share the gospel with him or her if the person is not a believer.

7. Offer better options.

8. Pray with the person (see 1 Peter 5:7).

9. Get a commitment from the person that he or she will not commit suicide or do anything

drastic. This small commitment can make a difference.

10. Tell the proper people.

Every state has its own legal requirements concerning the responsibility of the person who has knowledge of a potential suicide. You can find out your legal responsibilities from a pastor or a counselor. One thing to avoid is promising the suicidal person you will not tell anyone.

After the immediate crisis has passed, the real ministry of support begins. Do not assume that everything is now fine. The person needs support.

1. Be a friend and confidant (see the chapter on counseling).

2. Help the person find a Christian counselor because suicide is an indication of deeper issues. You are not a professional counselor, so help the person get counseling.

3. Work out a plan with the person.

4. Get him or her to make a pact with you that if he or she contemplates suicide again that he or she will call you immediately.

5. Decide on some positive things he or she can do like join a small-group Bible study, go to a worship service, read the Bible, and so forth.

6. Follow up with the person.

7. Pray for the person.

A Suicide Attempt

Many will attempt suicide but never actually succeed. Someone may have intervened and stopped it. Sometimes the attempt is a feigned attempt not meant to really succeed. Whatever reason for the failed attempt, you are now in a position to minister to the individual and the family after the attempt. Here are a few ways to minister to the person who attempted suicide:

1. Visit the person in the hospital, facility, or home.

2. Let the person know you love and care for him or her. At that point he or she is afraid of how people are going to respond to him or her.

3. Support the person (see the section on support under "Before a Suicide").

Minister to the loved ones of the person who attempted suicide. Oftentimes the loved ones are forgotten in the crisis. This is a crisis for them also. They may be in shock, frightened, or extremely angry. Take these steps to help:

1. Listen to them. You do not have to have all the answers.

2. Comfort them.

3. Pray with them.

4. Follow up with them.

After a Suicide

In this case the person has actually taken his or her life. The primary focus now is on the survivors, the ones who are left behind to deal with the issues. At this moment you are dealing with trauma. The reader should read the chapter on grief for more in-depth help.

Be with the survivors. Right now, more than anything they need your presence.

Listen to the survivors. They need to tell their stories. They need to vent their anger and ask their questions. A common response is anger. They will be angry with the person who committed suicide. "Why did he do this to me?" "How could she be so selfish?" and "I am so angry that he did this" are just a few of the responses you may hear.

Another common response is guilt. The survivors may blame themselves. "Why didn't I see this coming?" "If I hadn't yelled at him, he wouldn't have been so upset." "If I would have helped her, then she wouldn't have done this." "If I would have been there, I could have stopped him."

Do not feel like you have to answer all survivors' questions. Most of the time they are not looking for answers; they are just venting. Assure the survivors. They need hope. Their world is in shambles and chaos at that moment. Love the survivors. Mourn with the survivors (Rom. 12:15).

Nothing is as painful, shocking, and stressful as ministering during the midst of or in the wake of suicide. Sometimes you will be able to intervene and stop it, but sometimes you will not. Jesus reached out to Judas, but he refused Christ's invitation and took his own life. Your role is not to do the impossible but to love and care for the person as best you can. You must be careful not to assume guilt or blame if the person actually commits suicide. Be aware of your own grief and pain in the wake of a suicide.

Scripture

Anxiety and Fear: Matthew 6:25–34; Philippians 4:6–7; 1 Peter 5:7

Burdens: Psalm 68:19–20; Matthew 11:28–30

Comfort: Psalm 34:19, 20; 2 Corinthians 1:3–4; 7:6

God's Care: Isaiah 49:15, 16; Matthew 10:29–31

God's Help: Psalm 121; Isaiah 41:10; Hebrews 13:6

God's Love: John 3:16; Romans 8:39; 1 John 4:8*b*, 16; Jude 1:21

Hope: Psalms 33:18; 39:7; 42:1–11; 43:5; Romans 5:1–5; 15:4, 15; 1 Thessalonians 1:3; 2 Thessalonians 2:16; 1 Peter 1:3, 21

Suffering and Trials: 1 Corinthians 10:13; James 1:3–8; 1 Peter 5:10

Value of Life: Genesis 1:27; Exodus 20:13; Psalm 139:13–16; Matthew 6:25

Terminal Illness
Beth Chilcoat

[7] I have fought the good fight, I have finished the race, I have kept the faith. [8] Finally, there is laid up for me the crown of righteousness, which the Lord, the righteous Judge, will give to me on that Day, and not to me only but also to all who have loved His appearing.

—2 Timothy 4:7–8

Overview

When someone we care about is facing a terminal illness or dealing with the terminal illness of a loved one, knowing the "correct" thing to say and to do is quite challenging. We might wonder, "If I mention the illness, will she cry? If I don't mention it, will he think I am unsympathetic?" Naturally, we desire to ease the person's pain, but the fear of saying or doing the wrong thing can be paralyzing, so we often end up doing nothing.

I have had these questions myself, but I also understand things from the other side of this dilemma. When my fifty-five-year-old husband, David, and I learned that he had amyotrophic lateral sclerosis (ALS), a motor-neuron disease for which there is no treatment and no cure, we were suddenly thrust into the role of the "terminally ill." It was not a welcome experience. In fact, it would be difficult to overstate the devastation we felt.

The shock, grief, and magnitude of the loss we faced was overwhelming. Everything we had taken for granted, all of our assumed future plans, all of our earthly hopes, were brought to an abrupt and screeching halt. Soon we were immersed in the additional pain of watching our family, our friends, David's law firm, and our church as they reeled from the news as well.

What Is It Like to Be Terminally Ill?

The terminally ill patient experiences a barrage of emotions and challenges. Shock may be the first one, and this often leaves the person somewhat numb but in great anguish. Depression, panic, anxiety, and fear may all come into play. One is forced to grapple with many of the following issues:

- Physical concerns: pain and anticipated pain, grogginess from adjusting to medication, fatigue and constant physical demands, unwelcome physical changes and losses
- Financial concerns: inability to work long hours or not at all, increased debt due to medical costs, fear of incurring large debt for the family after death
- Family concerns: difficult or broken relationships, stress that this illness and loss places on children and other family members
- Spiritual concerns: fear of the unknown, questions about faith and why God is allowing this to happen

- Emotional concerns: crushing sense of loss, the desire not to leave loved ones, regrets and guilt

Ministry Strategy

When we learn that someone is terminally ill, we have two choices: to reach out in love or to draw back in fear or even indifference. Galatians 6:2 (NIV) instructs us to reach out, to "carry each other's burdens, and in this way you will fulfill the law of Christ." In James 1:5, God promises wisdom: "If any of you lacks wisdom, let him ask of God, who gives to all liberally and without reproach, and it will be given to him." If we are fearful, we can ask for His help in that as well because He has promised to equip us for the work He has called us to do (Heb. 13:21).

In practical terms, there are as many ways to minister to the terminally ill as there are terminally ill people. Each situation is different, and each stage of a disease presents its own distinct challenges. For example, every patient and every family has a unique personality and therefore different needs. Each day brings its own measure of pain and the subsequent ability to cope. In addition to these things, each family has its own level of spiritual experience and maturity. Some patients are not believers; others are believers dealing with unbelieving family members. Some patients are overwhelmed with visitors while others have no one coming to visit at all.

Despite these differences, however, David and I found some things to be helpful and some things that were not. I believe that two general principles provide a good starting place:

Take Your Cues from God (Prayer)

This is the believer's number one task and privilege. While many of us will remember to pray for the terminally ill patient—asking God for comfort, strength, and healing—we often set out to visit in our own strength. Prayer for ourselves is equally as important as prayer for the patient. We need to minister to others in God's strength and wisdom. He needs to impart His words and His comfort. Often we ask God to help the patient while telling Him, in effect, that we have got our part covered. If we go in God's strength rather than our own, we are better able to accomplish the second principle.

Take Your Cues from The Patient

Often the terminally ill are subject to increasing fatigue. The length of your visit should be determined by the needs and stamina of the patient, not the length of time you have allotted for the visit. For the same reason, always call ahead. But go, and keep in mind that we are the hands and feet of Christ and He calls us to visit the sick (Matt. 25:36–40).

How Can I Help the Person with a Terminal Illness?

There are many ways that you can help the patient and his or her family. In our case, acts of reaching out in a sensitive and caring way when we were feeling most vulnerable helped us to know that we would not face this journey alone.

Prayer was the first way people came alongside us and eased our way. Some would gather and pray with David for healing and strength. Some simply prayed on their own, but it was comforting to know that so many people were lifting our situation up to almighty God. Take your cue from the patient as to whether you will pray with him or her or just for him or her at a later time. Either way, prayer was the most important thing we received, and although David was not healed physically, we felt God's strength and guidance throughout the entire illness.

Unfortunately, there were a few visitors who implied that if we just had enough faith, David would be healed. Not only is this bad theology, it is also very unhelpful. Certainly God can heal, but these things are in His hands alone. Even an assurance that God will heal is hard to hear because the person wants so badly to believe that. Avoid assuring the person of physical healing; it just makes it harder in the end.

If the patient still has days when he or she is feeling well, offer to take him or her out and have some fun. At first, David's friends would take him golfing for brief periods since this was something he loved. Later, when he did not have the energy to actually play, he would just ride in the cart with them until he was tired.

If the patient is homebound, he or she may greatly appreciate a visit. But keep visits short and err on the side of brevity. Come more often for short periods of time rather than make rare long visits.

Be sensitive to the patient's needs. Listen to the patient. Long monologues by the visitor will wear out the patient. Take note of any specific needs he or she mentions and see if you can meet them. In addition to visiting, sending caring notes and cards is an encouragement. They help the person and the family not to feel so isolated. Bring along something helpful. If it is near a mealtime, and depending on the person's dietary restrictions, bring a light meal or a snack. The person may appreciate a good book. Perhaps you could lend the patient CDs or DVDs that he or she might enjoy.

Allow the patient to bring up hard subjects. Ask the person how he or she is doing but let him or her take the lead in what to discuss. Some days the individual may desire to share his or her grief and questions. At other times he or she may simply wish to talk about lighter subjects and not deal with the heavy stuff. My husband loved humor, and it helped him to be around people who would, in addition to praying with him and listening to him, make him laugh.

Toward the end of his illness, David could no longer turn himself over in bed. I could not do all the care twenty-four hours a day, and since time was short, I prayed that he would have people help him who really cared about him and were not strangers. This seemed like an impossible prayer, but God generously provided friends and family who took turns spending the night and helping him. This was such a witness to our neighbors and a priceless blessing to us.

Lastly, as God leads, share the wonderful assurances God gives to all who know Him: strength to get through each day, comfort in all situations, and, for all who believe, the absolute assurance of our heavenly dwelling place reserved for us in heaven. There were so many Scriptures that we found immensely helpful and comforting. They are listed below.

How Can I Help the Family?

Opportunities abound in this area. Families facing terminal illness are pulled in many different directions. The normal household duties remain, but added to them are care for the patient and all the extra errands and tasks that are required. Friends may minister in countless ways:

- grocery shopping
- bringing meals and organizing a schedule for meals (be sure to check on dietary restrictions first)
- house cleaning
- making phone calls
- running errands
- doing yard work
- babysitting
- driving children where they need to be
- helping with homework
- befriending older children and providing a safe

relationship where they can process their own concerns and grief

- doing laundry
- staying with the patient so the caregiver can get things done or just get a break
- being a nonjudgmental ear for the spouse or caregiver
- checking on sources for any equipment the patient might require (there are often wheelchairs and other needed items available on loan)
- fund-raising if there are large medical bills or other financial needs
- driving to therapy or doctors' appointments

Ministering to the terminally ill is our call and blessing, and it often strengthens us spiritually as well as brings us comfort. We need to take the opportunity to come alongside the terminally ill people God has placed in our path, asking Him to guide us and look for the blessings He brings.

Scripture

Comfort: Matthew 5:4

Fear and Anxiety: Philippians 4:6–7; Matthew 6:34; Hebrews 13:21

God's Love: Romans 8:35–39

God's Presence: Matthew 28:20*b*

Heaven: John 14:2–3

New Body: Philippians 3:20–21
Strength: Psalm 118:14
Visiting the Sick: Matthew 25:36–40
Wisdom: James 1:5

Part Four
Implementation

Developing a Ministry of Congregational Care
Richard Halcombe

There I was, wearing a blue surgical cap and matching paper gown, apprehension and excitement twisted into a tight knot in my stomach. I was not entirely certain I was ready to be a dad. Here we were, 1,100 miles from our closest relative, and my wife was delivering our first child five days before her due date. We were in Fort Worth, Texas, to pursue education for what God was calling us to do. We were part of a church at the time and enjoyed our connections there, but church was not the main wheel turning underneath that azure cap. How is this going to go? Is it going to be okay? Is my wife going to be all right? Will the baby be healthy? There were lots of questions void of answers. A nurse beckoned me to the lobby and I remember having a sick feeling in my stomach. People rarely ask you out of a room for good news. Walking out those double doors, apprehension turned to celebration when eleven people from our Sunday school class were there cheering as I walked out the door. The high fives and the hugs gave me security that no matter what the answers were, we were not going to have to answer them alone. Twenty-two years later, I smile every time I think about it. Tina and I were not alone in the world. Our biological family was at least a day away, but our church family was there. We knew that whatever the next few hours held, there were people who were holding us. That same group was the first to hear "It is a girl, and she is healthy!" Because those people cared about us, we knew and felt the church cared about us. And because the church cared about us, we knew God cared about us.

Within a year after our first child's birth, our phone rang with news of death. My only brother-in-law, at eighteen years of age, was tragically killed in an automobile accident. To that day, I had never personally experienced the depth of pain we felt. The angst was crushing, and barely bearable. It was a hole that would not be filled. That same church—our church—helped us financially and emotionally, to get through a time when my heart was falling out of my chest. They were there in the good times and bad, birth and death, breathtaking heights and oxygen-depleting depths. They stayed the course with us. She, the beautiful bride of Christ, was a church who loved us, a model for what any church can be and what church should be. The pastor's sermons were excellent. The facilities at the time were okay. The location was hard to find. But the caring relationships made it home.

Your church can be that church. A church that cares reflects the nature of the one who died for us and the one who calls us to do what He did, to care about other people. The Great Commandment tells us to do it and Christ's life shows us we should do it, but the question is, "How do we do it?"

The two main phases of developing a ministry of congregational care are the preparation phase and the implementation phase. Implementation will continue as long as the ministry does, whereas the preparation phase is like the first few minutes of the lift-off of a space shuttle. It will not take very long, but it will take more energy than it will take to sustain the journey.

Preparation

"Well begun is half done," Aristotle said. As with any undertaking, the preparation determines the success to a large degree. In my younger years working my way through college, I thought painting meant picking up a brush, sticking it in a can of paint, and starting on a wall. After a lot of time spent scrubbing paint off baseboards, and cleaning speckled floors and splotchy doors, I realized it would have taken less time to prepare than it would to clean up. And some things never did come totally clean. The same is true of ministry. Preparing well mitigates mopping up mistakes. In a nutshell, the principles of the preparation phase are to clarify the purpose, ensure support from your pastor, and encourage input from people.

Clarify the Purpose

The main reason we develop this ministry is to fulfill the message of Christ. To develop a ministry of congregational care means that your church, in a very practical way, will live the Great Commandment. In Matthew 22:37–39, Jesus tells us "'You shall love the Lord your God with all your heart, with all your soul, and with all your mind.' This is the first and great commandment. And the second is like it: 'You shall love your neighbor as yourself.'"

The purpose could be stated as "The purpose of the ministry of congregational care is for each member to sense a connection to, and care from, our church." This definition can be tweaked to represent more fully the heart of your church. It is a key, and a very necessary part, of discipleship. It shows the love Christ commands in the second part of the Great Commandment. And it is heartening and encouraging to all involved, whether you are a care group leader or a care receiver. And there is necessarily some room for flexibility in how this definition is lived. You will notice the purpose statement is:

- Universal: "Each member" proposes no one would fall through the cracks. This sets the level of expectation very high, in that no one in our church will feel isolated and uninvolved. It will take a load of work and thinking, doing, and trying. Remember the times you felt loved and people cared about you, and that will answer any questions about whether or not it is worth the effort. Additionally, only heaven can measure the results.
- Individual: The purpose says "each member to sense" because people sense care in different ways. Some appreciate a phone call; others would rather have a personal visit. It is important to operate the ministry in the way that each individual feels care, instead of the way the care group leader may feel care. If a care group leader is an outgoing, fun-loving,

my-life-is-an-open-book kind of person, it does not mean that the more quiet, introspective care receiver would enjoy a party. The care receiver, in this example, would probably enjoy a well-chosen card or a one-on-one personal visit. Since the point is that the person receiving care will feel care, go with what that person would want, rather than what others may prefer.

- Tethered: "Our church" means the ministry of congregation care is necessarily church-centric. There may be other programs and processes designed to help people in the larger community, yet the ministry of congregational care is the mechanism to care for the people God has connected to our church.

- Results-oriented: "For each member to sense a connection to, and care from, our church" shows the bottom line is for each member to sense a connection. There are a few things that make this harder than just having a checklist. The primary challenge is to know how people best sense connection. Some may feel connected, while some may sense it by being included in ministry or using their spiritual gifts. All of these should be considered when we consider the approach for particular individuals. So how would you measure this connectedness or know how it is going? One solid way to chart your progress is to give an

anonymous survey to all the members of the
church six months into the process.

Practically, developing a ministry of congregational
care means we will do the following:

Contact initially, as the ministry begins or when a
new member joins the church. This is a good time to
discover how to best care for the person, how he or she
would prefer to be contacted, and how often, along with
allowing you to share some life experiences to begin the
relationship.

Attend consistently, however often the leaders determine it should be. This is a good discussion for your care
group leaders. How often should we connect with people
in our group?

Respond quickly, when a need arises in the individual's life.

Encourage continually, as we "put courage in" one
another to follow the Lord and to live life for Him, no
matter what happens.

Enlist Pastoral Support

For any ministry of the church to do well, the pastor's support is needed. He is the primary representative
of the church and in most churches the key player for
every committee. Most pastors care about people. That
is part of the reason your pastor joined the ranks of the
clergy. Faced with myriad pressures, your pastor could
have lots of questions arise in his heart when you talk

to him about starting a ministry of congregational care. A few of the things he may be wondering are Does this mean I have not been doing my job well? Are people in the church thinking I have not been visiting them? Is there dissatisfaction with what is happening here? Do not be surprised if he is a little taken aback when you first broach the subject. Help him to see that the ministry of congregational care extends his ministry. Part of the training for people doing the ministry is to teach them to say, "Pastor (name) asked me to check on you, to see how you are doing." Affirm the pastor and how God is using him in your church. Be careful to communicate that just as God is using your pastor in your church, you want God to use you. Involve the pastor, as much as he desires, to be involved with the planning and the launching of the ministry. Unity in the church benefits a ministry of congregational care. Disunity in the church hinders it. For unity to persist in the body of Christ, the pastor needs to sense God's leading in it.

If you are the pastor, and you are the one initiating this ministry, congratulations. You see that God wants to touch and use many other people in your church. You recognize that one person cannot and should not do all the caring in the church. It is physically and practically impossible. In addition, if one person is doing the caring, several others are excluded from ministry and kept from experiencing the same joy and fulfillment you sense when calling on others. Just as God has gifted you, He has gifted others to minister, care, and call. And as people increase their personal responsibility for ministry, they feel more connected to the congregation as a whole. Oftentimes, they become more committed to the church and its other ministries because they are experiencing the positive work of the church firsthand.

Just as this ministry benefits the ones doing the calling, it is a blessing to the ones receiving the contacts. The homebound knows he or she has not been forgotten, and the people in crisis have been emotionally marked by the demonstrated love and consideration. The chronically ill senses he or she is still important to the church, and more important, still important to God. Done well, the ministry of congregational care is a win for everyone involved.

Encourage Input from People

After consulting with the pastor, a good approach is to talk to people in the church. Involve others in the preparation. Probably the strongest means of implementation for a ministry is to involve others in the preparation. People support what they help create.

Who is already calling on people? If you start a ministry of congregational care while someone feels he or she is already doing it, feelings could be hurt and the ministry could be hindered. Neither is desirable. If calls are already being made, let the callers know you appreciate what they are doing and offer those same opportunities to others. The people who are already doing the calls could offer invaluable help in getting the ministry launched, helping to provide training, and organizing the people they know who need care.

Another good way to assist the launch of a ministry is to have a formal means of moving forward. In some churches, this would mean a vote in a business meeting. Use whatever means your church typically uses for broad-based support. This is an important step, and usually comes at the point where there is a lot of understanding and involvement already. It is usually a mistake to begin by making a motion in a business meeting, and then trying to explain in those few minutes what the ministry of congregation care is. Many more questions are answered if the pastor and people begin working on the different aspects of the ministry before there is an official vote.

Another helpful idea, after people are trained and are ready to go, is to have a commissioning ceremony as part of a worship service. This may be at the end of a Sunday morning service where the care callers are asked to stand in front of the church. The pastor then prays for them and asks God to use them. This gives the callers the support of the church, and it also lets the church know that these are official representatives of God's body here. This may also help overcome the "head guy syndrome." Many church people think if the "head guy" has not visited them, they have not really had a visit. It takes time to wean people away from this faulty thinking, and a commissioning ceremony moves the thinking in the right direction.

Implementation

The ministry of congregational care will not look exactly the same in any two churches, and it should not look the same. You have different people involved, with varying gifts and strengths, and are in your own unique settings. Rather than giving particular rules to follow, focus on accomplishing the following key result areas. Each result area will be followed with an explanation of how this may look in your local context. The main result area is the same as the purpose: "for each member to sense a connection to, and care from, our church." So at the end of the day, if each person has sensed a connection to, and care from, your church, you have done your job.

Consider using the existing Sunday school/small-group structure. After all, the Sunday school/small-group ministry is the church organized to do the ministry of the church. Out of the ministries of your church, your Sunday school/small-group ministry (typically) has the largest group of leaders, the largest number of members, the largest sphere of influence, the highest potential for reaching the lost, and the largest opportunity for discipling the saved, along with the most horsepower to show care and concern to people in the church. It is not necessary to reinvent the wheel for people to feel love and care. It happens most naturally and most strongly in a structure that is already in place. This also helps avoid any pushback from those who do not want another "program" or who are resistant to a new thing they do not fully understand. Some general retooling to incorporate a care ministry typically meets more acceptance than a complete overhaul or a new ministry. If done outside of the existing structure, do not be surprised if the idea of a care ministry is met with suspicion, since the participants do not know how it will fit with what they are already doing.

If no Sunday school/small-group structure is in place, go through the normal protocol to begin it. This would include working with the pastor to see who would be candidates to receive care from the ministry. Ideally, every person would be assigned to someone. In a church where the membership roll has been around for a long time, a better option would be to include people who have attended within the last two years. Those people would form your list. And every person on that list would be assigned to a care group leader who would be responsible for that individual.

Ensure everyone in the organization is assigned to an individual. Avoid the mistake of assuming someone will pick up a name or a person in trauma. Stay with the system for the care coordinator to make the assignment and document when it was made. If everyone is responsible, no one is responsible.

Find the church membership roll or the Sunday school/small-group membership roll. Put a maximum of seven people (remember these are guidelines, and the exact numbers may vary) in any one person's group of people in a sphere of care. Try to balance each group where you will not have a lot of very needy people in any one group.

Develop expectations for the ministry. One main expectation is stated in the purpose. This ministry is for every person. The standard is "all." Every person is important to the Lord and we need to show each person he or she is important to us and to the church. Beyond "all," decide (alone or with church leaders) how often we should contact people. How often should each person get a contact? What kind of contact should each receive? There are a number of options for contacting, including making a personal visit; sending a card, letter, or e-mail; delivering cookies; and meeting for breakfast or coffee. Consider starting a Facebook page, with clear parameters. One parameter for Facebook or the church bulletin is not including anyone's name or information without his or her consent. In one church, a woman who had undergone an emotionally taxing, physically embarrassing procedure came to church and saw it posted in the church bulletin for all to see under the heading of "prayer concerns." She left that church.

Develop expectations for the ones who will be doing the calling. Should they be Christians? Church members? Active? Committed? What does it mean to be active and committed in your church? A good way to develop expectations is to involve the people in developing them. Gather the people (including the pastor if he desires) around a table. Give each person a packet of sticky notes. Ask each person to write one expectation on each sticky note. Write as many expectations as you can think of, but just write one per note. Ask each person to read his or her note as he or she hands it to you. Then stick it on the wall. After all notes have been read and stuck, ask the participants to stand. Direct them to approach the wall and group the notes in whatever groups they think fit together. If they see a note in one group, and it looks like it would fit better in another group, move the note. After a few minutes, the group will sort the proposed expectations. After the groupings have formed, invite the participants to go back to their seats. With their help, devise headings for each group. These headings then become your expectations for your leaders. Ask someone to type the information and get it to each participant later. As you bring onboard new ministry callers (care group leaders), share these expectations with them.

Building a Team

Recruit your team. A solid potential team of care providers would include people for a variety of roles, so the team functions well. A care coordinator is the key leader for the congregational care ministry in the church. This person is entrusted to see that the purpose is fulfilled. The main activities required are to recruit care group leaders, orient them to the ministry, and keep track of who has been contacted and who needs to be contacted. Depending on the size of the church, the care coordinator may need to recruit others to help with the responsibilities under this area. For example, you may recruit another person to track the visits and all the information that goes with it. Depending on the church, the care coordinator may also represent the church on the church council, church board, or some other group whose members oversee ministries of the church.

Each team should include care group leaders. These are the people who will do the connecting, the caring, and the calling. They are special agents of God's grace in the lives of those who receive them. Just as teaching or singing in the church requires work and training, the ministry of the care group leader also requires dedication and commitment. The ministry of care is vital to the healthy functioning of the local congregation. A good ratio is for each care group leader to have no more than seven in his or her group. In a couples' class/group, you might consider having a couple be the co-care group leaders for seven other couples. The care coordinator would recruit these care group leaders using the following method of "approach, apprentice, and applaud."

Approach

Pray first. Ask the Lord to show you who the next care group leader might be. Look for people who love the Lord and love people. Listen as people describe what they enjoy doing. Also keep your spiritual eyes open for someone who might want to get more involved with the church and ministry. If a person already is juggling several responsibilities (whether church-related or not), this might not be the best fit. If someone is already calling on people informally, he or she is a great candidate to be part of this ministry.

Apprentice

I will help you do something I would not feel comfortable or qualified to do on my own, and most other people are like that too. People prefer mentors to manuals. Make five visits with the person who wants to learn and has a heart for the Lord and people yet feels ill equipped for ministry.

Applaud

Celebrate and encourage the care group leaders you have apprenticed. Consider personal notes, words of encouragement, or recognition in the church bulletin. The behavior you reward is the behavior that will be repeated.

Establish a Monitored Feedback System

Decide how the care coordinator will track the people and the visits. There should be a column for the care group leader's name. Underneath her or his name would be all the people in her or his care group. The second column would be the date the assignment was made. Column three would be the date the care group leader made the contact (based on her or his returned report). Column four would include any special information. This is a sample. You may design a better feedback system. The main point is that you need one. Truth be told, this is the main weakness in most care ministries. People make contacts, or sometimes do not make contacts, but nobody checks to see. People do what you inspect, not what you expect. Set a standard for reporting the contacts the group made. It is best if the care group leaders report to you within twenty-four hours after the group member made the visit. If any of your callers do not have e-mail, they report the following Sunday. It is the responsibility of the care coordinator to contact the care group leaders when someone in their group has not been contacted. For most people, a contact once every month or two may work well. For others, especially those who are homebound, a weekly visit means a lot.

Train Workers

Provide skill development for your care group leaders. This is also a means of helping you to care for the care group leaders.

Making Contact

The care group leader makes initial contact. "Hi, this is Frank Johannson from the Grove City Church. I wanted to call and let you know I am your care group leader. Pastor Jesse wanted me to call and ask if you have any prayer requests." That is a good initial contact. From there, you can ask to meet the people and find out more about them. This is the first step in the CARE plan:

- Contact initially.
- Attend consistently.
- Respond quickly.
- Encourage continually.

Tips on Training

Now that the initial contact has been made, you are well on your way to achieving full implementation of the ministry of congregational care. It is important to be sensitive to the situations people face and not to treat everyone the same. The care coordinator and the care group leaders should have a cursory knowledge of the difference in sudden onset (acute) problems in people's lives, and how those differ from people who are in ongoing, (chronic) difficult situations. Remember, different needs need different deeds.

Dealing with Acute Situations

An acute situation is a smack, boom, whack of an event that only happens a few times in a lifetime (like the birth of a child). It can also be a sudden onset (like an injury or illness) or a devastating heartbreak (death of a family member or close friend). It is an episode in life unusual in time and/or unusual in intensity. Upon hearing about someone in your care group who has had an acute situation occur, a good strategy is go, flow, show.

Go

Go as soon as you hear about it, even if at 1 a.m. Go, even if the person says, "You do not need to come, I just wanted you to pray for me." If the person calls, you are wanted. The person may say he or she does not want you to come because he or she does not want to inconvenience you, or put you on the spot. But we know; if you get a call, the person wants you to come. If the caller did not want you to come, he or she would have waited until the next morning to place the call.

Flow

Upon arriving at the home, when you enter, greet everyone in the room. Look at each person as you do, and greet each with a solid handshake. This action provides warmth and security during unsettling situations. As you do this, pay special attention to the pace in the room. People generally move slowly and talk lowly when serious changes are occurring, as should you. It is important to adjust your pace to match the hurting family's pace. If they are sitting sullenly in a darkened room, sit with them and talk in a quiet voice. Sometimes it is best, especially in the presence of severe emotional pain, to sit quietly without speaking. If people in the room are chatting noisily and telling jokes, it is okay to be a little louder. The key principle here is to follow the pace instead of setting the pace. Following the pace builds rapport by helping people feel you are "with" them, which is a higher level of caring than just "being" there.

Show

Exemplify the caring compassion of Christ verbally and nonverbally. Show compassion. You may be wondering, What will I say? You really do not have to say anything. Your presence shows you care. You are involved, at the time of the crisis/acute event, in the "ministry of presence." The family knows there are bunches of other things you could be doing. They also know they are hurting emotionally and they do not want to be hurting, yet they have no choice. So for you to choose to enter a hurt, someone else's hurt, their hurt, when you do not have to have that hurt, makes them feel your care and love.

Choose Words Wisely

A pastor friend of mine was preaching a revival in another city. The pastor of the guest church asked him if he would like to visit someone who was about to have surgery. Of course he agreed. Upon finding the individual who was waiting in a preparation room for surgery, their pastoral visit began. The guest pastor said to the patient, "My uncle had the same kind of surgery you are about to have. As a matter of fact, it was in this same hospital. And, what is more interesting, his preoperational procedures were in this very room." Of course, the patient asked, "How did he do?" The pastor replied, "He never made it off the table," meaning the patient died while in surgery. This was not a good thing to share. Imagine the alarm, panic, and anxiety that patient felt. The pastor may not have known the patient would ask about the outcome when he told the story, but he should have known. Avoid stories that will predictably end with a scary result for the person who is supposed to be helped by the visit.

It also is best to avoid words that have the potential of being misunderstood, or worse, words that wound. The word *sarcasm* means "to cut." A caring visit is the last place to use sarcasm and definitely not an appropriate venue to give somebody a hard time. Those people are already having a hard time or you would not be there.

Even if you have known the distressed people for years, it is more effective to console rather than cajole. Speak in easily understood, comforting language. For example, you are in a room where a mother is in her final days after an extended illness. Her children are in the room, standing and quietly reminiscing about time well spent, a life well lived, and the pain of imminent separation. Avoid saying a statement like, "It does not look like anybody cares around here." No matter your intent, it can be hurtful as people wonder, What did he really mean by that? Does he really think we have not done all we could? Why would he say something like that? Sentences where words give a message other than the intended message compound the pain. Even if the hearers do know the intent, it forces them into several mental revolutions to get to that conclusion, something terribly unwelcome during terrible times. It is much more effective, and more caring to say something like, "It is wonderful how you have cared for your mother." That statement is straightforward, caring, and complimentary. It helps ease the pain of the passing by knowing they are doing what they can do, and you recognize their efforts. Remember, people respond to your content, not your intent.

Another rhetorical device to refrain from using is the cliché. These are well-worn phrases repeated often, which lack the individual element of the situation. "It will all be okay," may sound comforting, but it lacks insight. It lacks discretion about a little-known outcome. Your comment may be well-meaning but misplaced; maybe it will not all be okay. Too often the baby dies, the cancer continues, and the brain injury does irreparable damage. And even if the situation is okay for you, or would be okay for you if you were in that situation, it may very well not be okay for the person in that situation. It is better to use phrases backed by a beefier bottom line than to promise things you cannot know to be true. "I love you." "I care about you." "God loves you and no matter what happens, I will be here to help." Those are statements you know to be true, and give great comfort in times of stress. They carry authenticity and commitment, both of which are personified by the fact you are there with them in their time of need.

A good principle to follow when visiting someone is do not mention any information you have not heard directly from the person you are visiting. Typically, you will not know exactly what the ailing person knows. Furthermore, what you heard about the ailing person may or may not be accurate. Even if you received accurate information, you may not know all the reasons that the person's family or doctor have not shared the information with the patient. It is best not to offer information. Let the ailing person tell you. It not only saves you the embarrassment of saying something you should not say, it can be helpful for him or her to talk about it. But you also do not want to force the person to talk. A good question to use is to ask the person, "What are they telling you?" This leaves the patient free to discuss or not discuss what is happening. Since you left the word *they* open-ended, you allow the person being visited the dignity and option of saying what he or she chooses. This question uses only the information the patient already has, so the person in the bed is not shocked by something you say, which may or may not be true.

There are a number of ways to say the wrong things. These can be avoided by sitting yourself in the seat of the soul seeking solace. A good navigational tool for these situations is to ask yourself, What would I appreciate in my time of need? Words of encouragement, a hug or handshake, and someone being there are all solid solutions showing care for the hurting.

Dealing with Chronic Situations

A chronic situation is an ongoing, life-limiting situation, where the limitations become part of the normal rhythm of life. A person who is confined to home because of an extended illness or debility has chronic difficulties. The approach here is to offer ongoing support rather than an emergency room response. Taking tapes of the pastor's sermons to her or him, and reading to her or him from last week's (or next week's) Bible study lesson (from the class/group she or he would attend if able) are ways to help the homebound person stay connected and know that you care. And when you care, you are a present, particular, personal indication that God cares. When you go, you are God's representative to the person. When we attend church together, we see and experience many people who are showing the love of Christ. When you are the only one Christ's love is multiplied through you because you are the only one the debilitated person sees. You are Jesus in that living room or nursing home. Follow the same general guidelines as an acute situation, while making adjustments to the reality that chronic situations are going to be longer. In a chronic situation, you will build more of a relationship over time, and the person will probably look forward to your visits and will be expecting you.

Caring for Care Group Leaders

It is important to care for the people who are caring for others. Watch for signs of compassion fatigue. Signs include a lack of reporting visits, lessened energy for the ministry, and changes in behavior that would include being more sporadic in church attendance. All of these are cries for help, and the care coordinator is the one most tuned to hear these. It is important for the care coordinator to meet with the care group leaders on a regular basis, probably not more than monthly. Provide training (maybe using several of the ideas here) to help your callers meet their challenges. It is also a good idea to model to your care group leaders how you want them to meet the needs of the people they are contacting. When you see signs of compassion fatigue, it is your time to do the things you have been teaching. Meet individually over coffee with the care group leader who is hurting or check and see how the caller is doing.

Closing

As the ministry continues, the care coordinator adds new church members to the list of care groups. Care group leaders make the contacts and report whom they saw and when, and the pastor provides ongoing support to the care group leaders. This is an ever-strengthening system of support to encourage one another, to bear life's burdens, and to enjoy life together because we know relationships are the essence of life according to Jesus.

Endnotes

Part 1: Caring God's Way

1. Ralph H. Elliot, *The Message of Genesis* (St. Louis, MO; Bethany, 1962), 36. Elliot writes, "The two words are 'image' and 'likeness.' Linguistically, the word 'image' implies a hewn or carved statue or a 'copy' of something else while 'likeness' similarly means a facsimile. Thus, the words do not imply that man is divine. He is a copy after a divine one, patterned after a divine one with some of his attributes."

2. John Phillips, *Exploring the Psalms: Psalms 89–150* (Neptune, NJ: Loizeaux Brothers, 1988), 659–60.

3. Keith W. Sehnert, *Stess/Unstress* (Minneapolis: Augsburg, 1981), 38–39.

4. Rodney Stark, "Live Longer, Healthier and Better: The Untold Benefits of Becoming a Christian in the Ancient World," *Christian History and Biography*, January 1, 1998 (http://www.ctlibrary.com/ch/1998/issue57/57h028.html).

5. Tom Elliff, "Intimacy with God," audio recording of message presented to the Pastors' Conference of the Southern Baptist Convention, San Antonio, June 2007.

6. J. Oswald Sanders, *Spiritual Leadership*, 3rd ed. (Chicago: Moody, 1994), 29.

7. John C. Maxwell, *Developing the Leader Within You* (Nashville: Thomas Nelson, 1993), 39.

8. Joe Gibbs, *Racing to Win* (Sisters, OR: Multnomah, 2002), 183.

9. Avery Willis and Henry Blackaby, *On Mission with God* (Nashville: Broadman & Holman, 2002), v.

10. George Barna with Bill Dallas, *Master Leaders* (Brentwood, TN: BarnaBooks, 2009), 56.

11. James Merritt, Keynote speaker at the Southern Baptist Conservatives of Virginia State Convention, November 2001.

12. J. R. Miller, *Making the Most of Life* (New York: Thomas Y. Crowell, 1891), n.p.

Part 2: Caring for God's People

13. Howard Hendricks and William Hendricks, *As Iron Sharpens Iron: Building Character in a Mentoring Relationship* (Chicago: Moody, 1995), 131.

14. Bobby Clinton and Laura Raab, *Barnabas: Encouraging Exhorter, A Study in Mentoring* (Altadena, CA: Barnabas, 1997), 9.

15. J. Robert Clinton and Paul D. Stanley, *Connecting: The Mentoring Relationships You Need to Succeed in Life* (Colorado Springs: NavPress, 1992), 33.

16. Bobb Biehl, *Mentoring: Confidence in Finding a Mentor and Becoming One* (Nashville:

Broadman & Holman, 1996), 39–43.

17. Gary Mayes, "The Illusion of Mentoring," http://aboutleading.com/2008/12/04/the -illusion-of-mentoring, December 4, 2008.

18. Clinton and Stanley, *Connecting*, 198–208.

19. Terry Walling, *Focused Living Retreat Workbook* (Chicago: ChurchSmart, 2001), 42–49.

20. Avery Willis, *The Biblical Basis of Missions* (Nashville: Convention Press, 1979), 87–88.

21. Billy Graham, *Just As I Am: The Autobiography of Billy Graham* (New York: HarperCollins, 1997), 29.

Part 3: Caring for Hurting People

22. Ken Sande, *The Peacemaker: A Biblical Guide to Resolving Personal Conflict* (Grand Rapids: Baker, 2004), 29.

23. G. R. Collins, *Christian Counseling: A Comprehensive Guide*, 3rd ed. (Nashville: Thomas Nelson, 2006), 321.

24. Barna Group, *New Marriage and Divorce Statistics Released* (March 31, 2008), http://www.barna.org/barna-update/article/15-familykids/42-new-marriage-and-divorce -statistics-released?q=marriage+divorce +statistics+released.

25. G. R. Collins, *Christian Counseling: A Comprehensive Guide*, 3rd ed. (Nashville: Thomas Nelson, 2006), 609.

26. Linda J. Waite, Don Browning, William J.

Doherty, Maggie Gallagher, Ye Luo, and Scott M. Stanley, *Does Divorce Make People Happy? Findings from a Study of Unhappy Marriages* (New York: Institute of American Values, 2002), http://www.americanvalues.org/html /does_divorce_make_people_happy.html.

27. Andrew Cherlin, quoted in Pat Wingert, *Americans Marry Too Much*, Newsweek (August 15, 2009), http://www.newsweek.com /id/212140.

28. Raymond E. Vath, MD, *Counseling Those with Eating Disorders* (Dallas: Word, 1986), 36–37.

29. Ibid., 37.

30. Ibid., 32.

31. Herschel H. Hobbs, *The Life and Times of Jesus: A Contemporary Approach* (Grand Rapids: Zondervan, 1966), 180.

32. J. J. MacArthur, *The MacArthur Study Bible*, electronic ed. (Nashville: Word, 1997), Luke 22:44.

33. Granger E. Westberg, *Good Grief: A Constructive Approach to the Problem of Loss* (Minneapolis: Augsburg Fortress, 1997).

34. Elisabeth Kübler-Ross, *On Death and Dying* (New York: Scribner, 1997).

35. Substance Abuse and Mental Health Services Administration, *Results from the 2008 National Survey on Drug Use and Health: National Findings* (Rockville, MD: Office of Applied Studies, HSDUH Series H–36, HHS Publication

No. SMA 09–4434, 2009), http://www.oas
.samhsa.gov/nsduh/2k8nsduh/2k8results.cfm.

36. John Piper, "Ministering to Your Pastor,"
Desiring God Resource Library, http://www
.desiringgod.org/ResourceLibrary/Articles
/ByDate/1978/1786_Ministering_to_Your_
Pastor.

37. Adapted from Pastoral Care Inc., "Statistics,"
http://pastoralcareinc.com/WhyPastoralCare
/Statistics.php.

38. W. Wiersbe, *Be Faithful* (Wheaton, IL: Victor,
1988), 127.

39. Piper, "Ministering to Your Pastor."

40. http://bjs.ojp.usdoj.gov/index.cfm?ty
=tp&tid=11.

41. There is a complete Bible study of the
Nehemiah material and accountability in Mark
R. Laaser, *The L.I.F.E. Guide for Men* (Orlando:
Life Ministries, 2005).

42. Doug Rosenau, "Created by a Loving God,"
in *The Soul Care Bible* (Nashville: Thomas
Nelson, 2001), 7.

43. American Psychiatric Association, *Diagnostic
and Statistical Manual of Mental Disorders*,
4th ed. TR (text revision). (Washington, DC:
American Psychiatric Association, 2000). Both
substance abuse and dependence symptoms
can be located on pages 197–99.

44. Substance Abuse and Mental Health
Services Administration, *Results from the*

National Survey on Drug Use and Health: National Findings (Rockville, MD: Office of Applied Studies, NSDUH Series H–36, HHS Publications No. SMA 09–4434, 2009).

45. T. Clinton and R. Hawkins, *Biblical Counseling: A Quick Reference Guide* (Nashville: Thomas Nelson, 2007), 245.

46. W. Barclay, as cited in Chuck Swindoll, *Encourage Me* (Portland, OR: Multnomah, 1982), 49.

47. C. Swindoll, *Encourage Me* (Portland, OR: Multnomah, 1982), 54.

48. Centers for Disease Control and Prevention. Web-based Injury Statistics Query and Reporting System (WISQARS) [online] (2007). National Center for Injury Prevention and Control, CDC (producer), http://www.cdc.gov /injury/wisqars/index.html.

49. American Academy of Child and Adolescent Psychiatry, Facts for Family http://aacap.org /page.ww?name=Teen+Suicide&section=Facts +for+Families.

50. Friedrich Nietzsche, *Beyond Good and Evil: Prelude to a Philosophy of the Future*, trans. Helen Zimmern (New York: Macmillan, 1907), 98.

51. Friedrich Nietzsche, *The Gay Science*, ed. Bernard Williams; trans. Josefine Nauckhoff; poems trans. Adrian Del Caro (Cambridge: Cambridge University Press, 2001), xii, xvii, 108, 343.

Notes

Notes

Notes

Notes

Notes

Notes

Notes

Notes

Notes

Notes

Notes

Notes

Notes

Notes

Notes

Notes